Praise for *Profit F*

"Ronit's *Profit First for Salons* captures the absolute must-do's of not only running a profitable salon/spa—but overcoming the stress of debt and not having a life. If you're looking for a game plan for creating profit and rediscovering the joy of salon/spa ownership, read this book."

NEIL DUCOFF,
Founder of Strategies.com

"Driven by an unquenchable passion to serve, Ronit Enos is nothing short of remarkable. Since childhood, Ronit continues to break barriers by lifting up those around her. At times demanding, Ronit will reveal the few key metrics that will improve the profitability of your salon. *Profit First for Salons* is your map to achieving greater financial independence. Best of all, Ronit will be your guide, and there is no one better. Start your journey forward."

FRANK P. FULCO
CEO of Cosmetologists Chicago & America's Beauty Show

"Insightful, helpful, practical, and real. Trust it"

MR. ALOK APPADURAI
Founder of UpliftMillions.com

"Are you running your salon by the seat of your pants without a profit formula? Read *Profit First for Salons* by Ronit Enos and not only learn how to pay yourself first but also how to prosper without being tied to your chair!"

CANDY SHAW
Owner of Jamison Shaw Hairdressers, Creator / Founder of Sunlights Balayage

"Ronit is such a great leader, a good business person and so intelligent. She is generous, wise, very helpful, and shares her wisdom. You will love Ronit as a coach and you must read her book. Her mission is profit first for businesses and execution that really matters."

EVELINE CHARLES
Founder and CEO of Eveline Charles Salons | Spas | Beauty MD | Academy

"Salon owners have long been plagued by puny (or uncertain) profitability since I can remember (and I've been in this game for some time now). Leave it to Ronit Enos (via Mike Michalowicz' *Profit First*) to turn the current fiscal paradigm upside down using not only an innovative, but highly effective, proven formula to ensure salon profitability. Not to be mistaken as a theory, this is a message no salon owner should miss. Big thanks to Ronit for sharing her research and experience-based expertise with the beauty industry at large!"

TERRENCE "TERRY" MCKEE
Co-Owner, President and CIO (Chief Innovation Officer) of NUOVO Salon Group, and Secretary of Intercoiffure America Canada

"Sometimes, very rarely a book comes along and a new way of thinking appears that is a game changer for our industry. It is crackling with clarity and tingling with electricity of new ideas and methods for implementing them. Ronit has planted herself in the first rank of beauty industry books. It is thought provoking and creates what seems like an infinity of ideas to explore. It forces us to question conventional practices and create new strategies to build stronger, more profitable and sustainable businesses."

LEON ALEXANDER PH.D.
CEO and President of Eurisko Design

"Holy moly, people! *Profit First for Salons* will change your entire perspective on running a successful salon and give you an incredible, sustainable tool to take control of your salon and your finances starting day one. Ronit knows that a healthy salon leads to freedom, and it's obvious in this read she knows YOU are capable of the life you're dreaming."

ERIN MOGER
Strategic Guide at Profit First Professionals

"This is the *Rosetta Stone* for salon, spa, or barbershop owners. If you are looking for financial clarity within your business, this book is for you. If you are looking to pay yourself (more), this book is for you! If you are struggling with generating a profit, this book is for you! Ronit's book and programs create clarity, empowerment, and focus for all salon, spa, and barbershops."

RON SAHARYAN
Co-founder of Profit First Professionals

"This needs to be on the bedside table of every salon owner or stylist aspiring to be one."

RONAN PERCEVAL
Founder of Phorest Software

"Ronit has great enthusiasm, a deep desire to help, a good sense of humor, and all that is wrapped in fearless reflections. Based on her many years of experience, she generously shares her way to success. She learned from academic and real-life lessons. Her vivid story-filled writing can help salon owners be more successful by planning and controlling their financial management. A noble goal, and Ronit did a fantastic job."

VIKTORIA DALKO, PHD
Member of the Academic Board and Professor of Finance,
Hult International Business School

"Finances require a specific mindset. Find that mindset and the profits will follow. Ronit simply and understandably delivers a proven, easy to implement, step-by-step approach to build the thinking, emotions, and behaviors that create consistent and sustainable profits that allow you to take financial (and mental) control of your business."

JAY WILLIAMS
Author of *This vs That* and *Leave your Mark*

Profit First for Salons is a gift to all salon, spa, and barbershop owners who want to reclaim the joy they envisioned when they first opened their businesses. Ronit takes the mystique out of how to make and manage money so you can enjoy the life you've always dreamed of living.

KAREN GORDON
J. Gordon Designs & Karen Gordon Hair Loss Solutions

"What would your life be like if you could plan and count on the amount of profit you'll take home each month? If you could count on that, how would your life change? This simple system can turn your business around and help you start living out your personal goals. What are you waiting for?"

STACEY SOBLE
Director of Brand Content Strategy – SALON TODAY

"Simplicity is today's brilliance and *Profit First for Salons* is a must-read for every salon, spa, barbershop owner who desires to maximize their profits with minimum effort and create the life experience every owner desires."

SAM VILLA
Co-Founder of Sam Villa/Redken Global Artistic Ambassador

"Change your life today. Don't gamble on the future, act now, without delay." - Simone de Beauvoir.

PROFIT FIRST

—— *FOR* ——

SALONS

TRANSFORM YOUR BEAUTY BUSINESS FROM A CASH-EATING MONSTER TO A MONEY-MAKING MACHINE

RONIT ENOS

1. Small Business - Finance   2. Success in Business

Published by Merack Publishing

Printed in the United States of America
First Edition
This book is not intended as a substitute for financial advice.

ISBN: Paperback 978-1-957048-35-2
ISBN: Hardcover 978-1-957048-37-6
ISBN: eBook 978-1-957048-36-9

DEDICATION

Bill is the reason why this book has come to life. He is my rock, fan, and best friend. He understands why I am so passionate about sharing our experience with my community, including bringing this "magical" cash flow system into the world of beauty.

Both Bill and I have dedicated over 17 years to building our salons and committing to making them successful. Bill is my partner through the journey of our salon life and now in our training company, Salon Cadence. He has been living the *Profit First* Lifestyle with me all these years, from just starting - to using it full-out. I couldn't have done this without you, Bill!

CONTENTS

FOREWORD
BY MIKE MICHALOWICZ

The view was gorgeous. For them, but for me also. Ronit Enos and her husband Bill hopped on a call with me to discuss how they were helping struggling salon owners become permanently profitable. The window behind the desk they were sitting at revealed one of the most beautiful mountain views I have ever seen.

Instead of starting with the usual "How are things going?" I said, "My gosh, where is your office? That view is stunning!"

Ronit responded with "Well, today we are in Yellowstone National Park. We think we are going to head further west in a few days." That's my kind of office! Breathtaking views and the freedom to do what you want, when you want.

Ronit, Bill, and their two dogs were spending a few months, or longer if they decided, traveling in their Airstream across the country. That is when it struck me. Ronit, the author of *Profit First for Salons* is living the life that she creates for others. She has the financial and personal freedom to live life on her terms, and when you read this book, you will too.

As a salon owner you have an unsustainable "either/or" challenge, or so it seems. You need to put every ounce of your soul into the business, or you can have some time with your family. But you can't have both. In other words: You can enjoy money, but only if you don't enjoy life. At least that is what I heard from the countless salon owners I have met.

But Ronit's story was different, both for herself and the people she serves. You can have a business that fuels you. You can have financial freedom. And you can have the personal freedom to do what you want, when you want. But to do that, it must start with a simple, powerful system. You must take your profit first.

Ronit was not always living the life of financial and personal freedom. She too struggled. In fact, you will discover her whole story in the book. But let me give you a teaser. Ronit worked endless nights. Ronit missed family events. Ronit didn't see the sun rise or the sun set, because she was always pushing harder for just... one... more... day. And then, at the end of the month, after an exhausting effort there was nothing left. Not a single extra penny.

She sacrificed her family and her life for money, and yet there was none. She tried everything, and nothing moved the needle, until she discovered Profit First. With the simple system her life was transformed. She made money and made time. Balance came back and money poured in. Even a very notably beautiful Airstream became a quick reality.

And she discovered one more thing in her process of implementing Profit First, there were powerful tweaks she could make to the system. She added parts that better served her salon business. She removed parts that added little value. In a short time, she had enhanced the system so effectively for salon owners, that her colleagues wanted the system for themselves. Other salon owners started following Ronit's *Profit First for Salons* process, and they saw the same results. More time. More money. That is when it became clear Ronit was onto a bigger mission: Every salon owner needed this knowledge. Every salon owner needed Profit

First customized to them. That is why she wrote this book. That is why this book will transform your life.

If you have not met Ronit yet, let me do the honors of an introduction. Ronit Enos is a visionary strategist who teaches salon business owners to transform their passion into a money making machine. But she is more than "just" that, she is raw energy and enthusiasm in the purist form. Ronit grew her own salon, Maxime Brands, into a seven figure business, posting six figure profits. Her work has been featured in *Salon Today*, *Aveda Means Business* and *Authority* magazine.

Ronit is also the creator of Salon Cadence, an online community and coaching organization for salon owners. Salon Cadence has helped generate over $2.5M in net profits for the members and has empowered the community to experience a life of personal freedom.

I suspect your salon business is about to achieve your vision for personal and financial freedom. The path forward is simple, just follow the steps outlined in this book. Sit back, run a comb through your hair (that is salon owner code for: "Let's do this!") and read. Your salon and your life is about to be transformed.

HOW TO USE THIS BOOK

It saddens me to know that many people who pick up this book will read it all the way through, thinking how spectacular the concepts are, only to set it down and never think about it again. Don't get me wrong—they will have every good intention of coming back to execute the strategy, but life will get busy, and they'll tell themselves they don't have time right now and they'll come back to it later, but most never will.

Please, don't be one of those people! A working knowledge of what is possible by making some changes won't do anything for your salon or spa business. You'll be exactly where you started if you look at this book as just another learning experience.

Because I wrote this to change businesses and lives, I've designed it to be a step-by-step guide that you can implement each step of the way. Applying the system in this way will make it easier–you'll have less resistance to the changes, and you won't feel overwhelmed by it all.

I promise you, it's a simple process, but it *is* a process. It will take some time to get everything in place. That's not a problem! You will start seeing significant results even by implementing a few beginning practices. These fantastic results will motivate you to do more until you have a salon business that is beyond profitable before you know it. It will make your dream lifestyle a reality.

In the beginning chapters, I cover the WHY behind the system. You can't fully understand the tactics we'll discuss later in the book if you don't "get" the strategy behind it. After that, I've broken the Profit First system down into bite-sized "how to" chunks so you can use it like a workbook. I've held nothing back. I'm going to walk you through exactly what I did to turn my cash-eating monster into a money-making machine. I've included my story and some from my coaching clients to inspire you. I want you to see that *we are no different from you–if we could do it, so could you!*

To support you even further, I designed a website where you can find all sorts of free resources to make implementing *Profit First* even easier. I'll remind you throughout the book when there's a resource available on the site, so you get the very best I have to offer. If you want to take a sneak peek, go to ProfitFirstSalons.com.

Finally, since I love nothing more than championing other salon owners, I've created a free support group just for you. It's a safe, welcoming community where salon owners can get their questions answered by others applying the *Profit First* method to their businesses. You'll be able to connect with outstanding experts at the top of the industry who are serious about helping others become financially free, just as they are now. Again, you can find this and other resources at ProfitFirstSalons.com.

INTRODUCTION

"The number one thing I wish I could have while running my business is the energy to enjoy two hours at the movies with my daughter and not fall asleep."

Scanning the room, I saw looks of anguish and understanding on every face.

I recognized the look. I'd seen it for years whenever I'd looked in the mirror.

How many ball games and dance recitals had I missed while my children were growing up? How many occasions with my family had I slept walked through because my brain was lost in work—how was I going to keep my salon afloat?

Gee Jackson, a barbershop owner in Fairbanks, Alaska, went on to explain that he'd recently taken his young daughter to the movies for a couple of hours of daddy-daughter time. He'd been looking forward to the day because he never took an afternoon off from his business. It was a special treat for them both.

When the final credits rolled, Gee woke with a start, shocked that he'd slept through most of the movie. He was so worn out from running his business that he couldn't even stay awake for something he'd been anticipating. How many other ways had he been emotionally unavailable for his family?

Even worse, Gee confessed, he was working his fingers to the bone yet wasn't earning the income to show for it. He didn't have enough time or money to enjoy life with his family no matter what he did.

I met Gee when I was speaking in Fairbanks. I'd been thrilled and honored to be invited by Scott Allison, a client who'd made extraordinary strides in his business in the short three months we'd been working together, to speak about *Profit First*.

Sixty barbers, stylists, salon, and local business owners had gathered to learn how they could transform their profitability. As the afternoon wore on, I couldn't help noticing Gee's reactions to each phase of my presentation. Gee confirmed what I already knew to be true at the end of our day together. He couldn't hold back his excitement. His voice shook the room, "I can't believe how simple this is! I can do this. I *have to* do this!"

Gee realized that day that not only could he start to predict his income and profits by using a simple, logical system, but that he would no longer have to spend all those hours in the shop to earn the income he wanted for his family's lifestyle.

Gee's story touched me so profoundly because I'd been there. All those hours at my salon. The weekends. The missed family moments that I would never get back. Night after night, dragging myself home at nine or ten o'clock after a long day. I was exhausted and sick of the struggle of working so hard, only to bring home peanuts. Even more frustrating was that I knew the salon was bringing in good money, but at the end of the month, there was nothing left for me.

It was the same thing every day. Coming home, tired, overworked, missed dinners with my kids, missed time with my husband. I was so emotionally drained when I was home that I was no fun to be around. I'd be miles away, wracking my brain to figure out how I could turn my business around.

So, what did I do? (Gee did it too.) I worked more, spent more, added more hours to my schedule, generated more sales, and got more clients. I did everything I could to bring in more revenue. I squeezed as many sales from our salon clients as possible. I up-sold everything—extra services, retail promotions, gift cards, 2-for-1 promotions, VIP programs. I raised my prices and shortened service times.

But even after implementing all those strategies, it didn't matter because nothing had changed. I still couldn't take the paycheck that I deserved. I still worked so hard and late every day to barely cover our expenses. This wasn't the vision I had for myself when I opened my salon.

Desperate, I finally admitted to myself that I didn't know the fundamentals of running a business. I gathered resources and immersed myself in education on how to run a business. I read stacks of business books, participated in every workshop I could find, and hired four or five different coaches over several years.

And it paid off. I learned a tremendous amount about running a business. Finally, I understood financials, management, leadership, hiring, branding, and marketing. I learned how to put systems in place to automate my processes. But even with all I'd learned, I knew I was still doing something fundamentally wrong. I had a better handle on the business, but the profits I wanted still weren't there.

After all that hard work, I realized that no matter how systemized I was, how great my team was, or how exceptional my salon's reputation was, the only thing that mattered was if my business was generating profit. Even with the best systems in place, the best marketing and branding, and tons of traffic to our salon, it finally sunk in that I wouldn't have a business if I didn't become profitable soon. That reality has ultimately led me here to you.

The Glamour of Business Ownership

Salon owners are the ultimate entrepreneurs. We are filled with passion and dedication for the incredible vision we want to forge creatively and in our businesses. Most of us start our careers as stylists, developing our skills on the creative side of the business. We build tremendous value for our clients and often get to know them personally. We are quick learners who thrive on education and adopting new techniques. Some are wildly creative, while others love the concepts and become masters at the fundamentals.

Because we are creative people who need to grow and try new things, somewhere along the way, a shift occurs. As stylists, we begin to consider the next step in our career. We may become educators or ambassadors for a beloved product line. We may choose to take on a management role in the salon or move to another shop for new inspiration.

Then, there are the few of us who decide to own our own business. Thoughts of making our own choices, having money and time freedom, being more artistic, and serving our clients based on our values dance around in our heads until we feel we don't have a choice—we must become salon owners.

Dazzled by all the exhilaration, we go for it. We create a business plan, name, and logo. We build a website, incorporate the business, borrow money, design our space, enlist other stylists, hire a receptionist, reach out to clients, and launch a grand opening.

For the first six months, the buzz around us is addicting. Friends and family come to see our new space. We get a lot of great support and encouragement. Everything is new, so clients are excited for us, and there's traffic coming to the salon. New customers and stylists want to hear about our services and opportunities.

There is a great feeling of accomplishment. After all, it was a lot of work to get everything ready and make the transition. Many things popped up unexpectedly, but we dealt with them and got through it. We should be proud of this achievement. Nobody really understands the stress and anxiety that comes with opening a salon.

As time goes on, reality comes knocking on the door. Opening the salon was just the beginning of a long journey. We took the first giant step, but it's not the toughest. Now, we must run a company. We quickly realize that owning a business is much different than we envisioned.

Now, we have to think like business owners. Suddenly, banking, interviewing, hiring, training, compensation, taxes, inventory, cash flow management, marketing, and outsourcing are part of our daily life— our daily headache.

All these things start coming at us nonstop, and they all require cash. So, we do the only thing we can do… work! We work like crazy, putting in long hours, weekends, working on our days off. We spend more and more hours behind the chair just to stay afloat. It becomes a constant cycle that never stops, and there doesn't seem to be an end in sight.

Is There Any Light at The End of This Tunnel?

Sounds pretty grim, right?

But actually, there is good news. It doesn't have to be that way. As a salon owner, I believe that your business can serve YOU to the same level and depth you serve your clients. You can take back control of your business and NOT be controlled by it!

I work every day with salon owners who feel frustrated, unprofitable, burnt-out, overwhelmed, and trapped in the cycle of running a business. No matter what they do, how many systems they put in place or books they read and implement, they still feel there is never enough time to get everything done. When they're working in the salon, they feel like they should be at home with their families. When at home, they feel like they should be at the salon with their team and clients.

Many salon and spa owners think that a stressful, unfulfilled life is simply part of the "entrepreneurial normal" with all its ups and downs and never-ending craziness. That's just not the case. No matter what your story is, you can rewrite it with purpose and design to achieve the goals that matter to you. You can build a road map that allows you to take complete control of your business. All this is achievable by implementing a few key concepts which are the foundation of any thriving business.

Just because our cosmetology training didn't prepare us for running a business doesn't mean we can't! Your business doesn't have to be your most significant source of stress. You don't have to live hand-to-mouth as a salon owner. And you don't have to feel like a failure or worry if you are making the right decisions.

However, your situation will never improve until you shift your way of thinking as a technician to the mindset of a CEO and implement a few core principles that will allow you to build more wealth and create a company that can almost run itself. You need a business model designed to plan for profits and create a solid foundation for your company. A model that you can quickly and consistently learn, follow, and maintain.

Profit First for Salons is that foundation. Once you have the methodology you'll learn in this book, you will layer one system after the next to grow and thrive. Everything you do will be connected to your profitability. I can't wait until you get that breakthrough moment and see how it all connects! *Profit First for Salons* will allow you to transform your beauty business from a cash-eating monster into a money-making machine. It will free you to become the CEO of your life!

I Created a Profit First Business... And So Can YOU

I was first introduced to *Profit First* and Michael Michalowicz when I read *The Toilet Paper Entrepreneur (TPE)*. That book really hit home with me, and suddenly everything seemed to make perfect sense. It was like Mike was speaking to me directly. I learned a lot from the *TPE*, but the big lightbulb moment was when I realized I wasn't managing my money correctly.

In *The Toilet Paper Entrepreneur*, a small section lays out the basic foundation of his next book, *Profit First*. When I read that *Profit First* section, I knew I needed to do something completely different right away. I immediately did my best to implement the basics of *Profit First* in my salon, and I committed to the methodology even though the book hadn't been published yet. Once I started applying it, I started seeing a positive change in just a short time.

Even though I was taking baby steps, my savings account grew for the first time in years. Soon I was dictating exactly how I wanted to use the revenue and how much I wanted to earn each month. Finally, I could afford to pay off my debt. I was able to bring home the paycheck that I'd dreamt of because I'd created a *Profit First* company.

I'll never forget my first big win after committing to the *Profit First* system. I'd always wanted to take my team to Serious Business, a big salon education event in New Orleans. It would cost me $11,000 to do that, but I made it a priority. Using the *Profit First* methodology, I created a separate account and started putting a small percentage of every sale into it. Long story short, I was able to fly my team to a four-day retreat of world-class learning because I had that money saved specifically for that purpose. It was the best feeling in the world! And that is just the first of many stories I could tell you about how *Profit First* changed my life.

So often, salon owners spend 40+ hours a week behind the chair working to pay bills while missing opportunities to do the things that would make them happy and fulfilled. This book is written for those salon owners and independent stylists who want to control their businesses and work by design. It shows you how to build your entire financial system on a *common-sense* money method that works.

It will give you the peace of mind to focus on your vision and stop making knee-jerk business decisions based on money scarcity. You'll finally fall right to sleep at night without worrying about payroll or whether you can pay your quarterly taxes. You will know what to spend your money on, and you will have the financials to do it.

The most important thing is that you will have steady and consistent income growth without working even more hours. You'll have the confidence to handle hard times, such as COVID-19, market crashes, and other unpredictable events. You'll build your business based on *cash flow, not cash poverty.* Once you take action on the recommendations in this book, you'll be able to turn your vision into a reality, both for you and for those whose lives you want to positively impact.

And, What About Gee?

One of the things I love most about our industry is the inspiration I get from people I meet along the way. It took traveling to Fairbanks, Alaska, to meet Gee, but that chance meeting profoundly impacted me and my coaching business.

At the age of 23, Gee was sentenced to 10 years in federal prison. His life had taken a serious turn and sent him down the path of the unknown. We all have moments where adversity challenges us and puts life to the test. Meeting Gee and hearing his story was the ultimate example of this.

After a few years into Gee's prison term, he was introduced to barbering. It's not uncommon that inmates are given a chance to learn a trade, and barbering spoke to Gee. He quickly latched on to the opportunity and developed his newly found craft. Like most stylists and barbers, Gee experienced an intense level of confidence and fulfillment in his work.

During his time in prison, Gee imagined what it would be like to have his own barbershop. Even better, to be able to provide job opportunities for other men coming out of prison who were looking for a way to build a new life for themselves. He was determined to make that dream a reality, and he imagined it every day until his release in January 2013. Within weeks of his release, he enrolled in barber school, and exactly nine months later, he graduated and went to work on his vision of opening his own shop.

When I met Gee, he was in the process of launching his second location. We spoke at great length, and by the end of the night, he had become my first barbershop client. I was excited because I could see the passion and conviction he had to create the lifestyle business he wanted for himself and help as many others as possible to find their purpose and direction in life.

I worked with Gee for over a year, and during that time, he completely redesigned his business to run according to *Profit First*. He became the ultimate student and implemented every detail into his business. Within a year, he was building profits and expanding his team. More importantly, he was running his business according to how he wanted to live his life.

What impresses me most about Gee's success is how he took everything he learned through *Profit First* and combined it with his mission of mentoring people looking for a second chance. He teaches his team that it's not just about making money; it's about making sure that your money is working for you.

Thanks to *Profit First for Salons,* and Gee's powerful vision, he is now living his dream. He has four thriving locations in Alaska and Arizona, and he is working on opening his fifth. He owns two homes, so he's able to travel back and forth, and both of his sons have joined the company. His goal was to build a business aligned with his vision of impacting the lives of others, to help and teach people who want to be in control of their lives, not the other way around.

We recently caught up on the phone, and I asked Gee if he's seen any good movies lately. He said, with a chuckle, "Ronit, my daughter and I are watching them all."

CHAPTER 1

THE STARVING STYLIST

"Whenever you feel under pressure, crushed, or in fear, you are in a powerful place of transformation. Trust the process!"
– Dr. Leon Alexander

Over the years, I have met thousands of hairdressers and beauty professionals. As I think about all these fantastic people, there is one thing we all seem to have in common—the one simple unwritten rule that is engraved deep into our psyche. When we need more money, we immediately focus on getting more clients.

Just think about that for a minute. If you are a beautician and need more money, it seems logical that you should work to increase your clientele, and so that's what we do. We put all our efforts into growing our book of clients. I don't think this concept is something we were necessarily taught. It's just the way we're built. We believe more clients will equal more money.

Now, while it's true that more clients and services will bring more revenue, more revenue doesn't necessarily put more money in your pocket. Okay, maybe you'll see a quick burst of extra money in the short term, but here's the challenge: It just isn't sustainable. Selling your time has a cap to it, with a nice reward called "burnout" at the end of it. Our coaching company has a presentation on the Burnout Model concept (more about this in Chapter 9).

I lived in the burnout zone back in my early days as a stylist. In fact, I was so good at operating this way that I infused it into my business when I became a salon owner. I pushed my team endlessly to get busier while delivering excellent service. I believed the path to growth and success was more sales, more services, and more hours behind the chair. This was my formula for making money, and it took me several years to finally realize this way of thinking was a recipe for disaster.

Don't get me wrong, we are in the service industry, and we need clients to stay in business. For sure, income starts with sales and services, but for some reason, we get stuck on this idea that we have to keep growing and bringing in more and more sales to be successful. This belief leads us into becoming Starving Stylists.

See if you recognize the life cycle of The Starving Stylist:

You graduate from cosmetology school with a dream of having great clients and creating beautiful hair. You are hungry to learn, and your passion is at an all-time high. You think about all the money you're going to make once you have a solid list of regular clients, so your first step is to get out there and find a great salon and team to join.

As time goes by, you build a promising career for yourself. You're working steadily and gradually building your clients. You keep learning and improving your techniques. Before long, you start bringing home some good paychecks, and you're finally able to spend money on things for yourself. Maybe you buy a new car because now you can afford a car payment. You deserve nice clothes, so you get a credit card and make a few charges. Now you want a nicer apartment to match the new car and clothes. You make enough money to start enjoying finer restaurants and hitting the clubs with your friends.

This is how you evolve, and it's normal. You're young, excited, and willing to do the work so you can have these things, but here's the problem: Your income is based on selling your time. These new expenses require more money and a growing income. You're spending money in exchange for more time behind the chair, and you're doing this without a way of managing your money or knowing where your money is going.

The cycle continues, and you get another credit card. Perhaps you buy a house and start a family. Of course, you want to travel and experience memorable vacations. No problem, you can charge it and just squeeze in a few more clients each week to cover the costs. Your "burnout" system is working perfectly. You get good at spending money and paying for it with your time.

Before you know it, you're maxed out. You can't work more hours than you already have scheduled. You're exhausted, and your back and knees constantly ache from spending so much time on your feet. If anything, you'd like to reduce your hours, but slowing down is not an option. You have bills to pay. Your debt has taken on a life of its own.

For those of you who make the jump from stylist to salon owner, these challenges just got super sized. Now you get to keep working like a superhero, plus take on a bunch of new expenses and responsibilities. Mix it all together, and you have just created the perfect "burnout" recipe.

My Starving Stylist Story

How do I know this to be true? Because that was me! Yep, I did it all. I ran my salon from behind the chair. I was the primary producer, working 50 hours a week on clients, barely covering all my business expenses. What I earned didn't cover my personal expenses. I spent money like crazy in the salon. I constantly put money into things like marketing, hiring, products, equipment, education, and a premium location with high rent… all so I could bring more clients in to get more income. This is how you grow a successful salon business, right?

It may sound like I had a thriving business and was making tons of money, but the truth is that everyone was getting paid except me. After all the expenses and payroll were covered at the end of the month, I got nothing. I was working 70 to 80 hours per week with nothing to show for it. My costs were too high, and I was doing hair full-time just to keep my head above water. In addition, my stress level was off the charts.

I was entirely on my own trying to run a business as a full-time hairdresser. My list of duties included educator, hiring manager, marketing specialist, financial officer, event planner, payroll manager, team cheerleader, and the list goes on. I even learned the roles of plumber, electrician, and handyman. Everything that had to do with running a salon completely fell on my shoulders—all while being a full-time hairdresser.

But still, I kept the burnout cycle going. I thought if I worked 24/7 that I'd be successful. I believed if I just worked more and harder than everyone else, I would have better results and eventually have more time to invest in myself. If I controlled everything in my salon and micromanaged my employees to deliver extraordinary results, then everything would work itself out. If I could fill all my chairs, no matter what the cost, that's all I would need to be prosperous. I just needed to upsell my clients and teach my team to upsell, and that was all we needed to do. I only needed to borrow *a little more money* from my credit cards or personal savings to invest in marketing to attract more clients and staff. This became my life, day after day, month after month, for years.

I knew I was losing money. In fact, I was taking on new debt every month. Not only did we have a second mortgage on our house from opening the salon, now I was using credit cards to keep it going. I remember feeling like a victim—no matter how hard I worked, I just couldn't catch a break.

I was at my lowest point financially, emotionally, and physically. It seemed like everything was falling apart. I didn't have time for exercise. I was gaining weight, eating poorly, and compromising my relationship with my children and husband. I had become wholly starved for everything good I had set out to accomplish when I got into this business. I had become the poster child of The Starving Stylist.

The Recital That Changed My Life

One Saturday morning, it all came crashing down. I had just walked into my salon and sat at the front desk to check my staff's schedules. At that moment, I got a call from my husband reminding me that the recital started at 11 a.m. and not to be late. His words hit me like a Bruce Lee kick to the stomach. My whole body went completely numb. This was the long-awaited day of my daughter's cello tryouts at the New England Conservatory.

I had planned on blocking off my day at 10 a.m. to meet my family at the recital, but I'd completely forgotten. I had back-to-back clients all day long. Such an important moment in my daughter's life had suddenly been snatched away from me. I spent that whole Saturday at the salon while my daughter had the most amazing and successful audition imaginable. This was the ultimate low point—the moment I realized that my business was in complete control of my life. If I didn't make some profound changes, and quickly, I could kiss all my years of work, vision, and dreams goodbye. I felt like a total failure.

Most successful entrepreneurs have a moment like this. We seem only to be able to take a step back and look at the big picture once we've hit bottom. It took missing out on my kid's childhoods to realize I'd become a slave to my business.

After the missed recital, I confessed to my husband, Bill, over dinner after a long, busy day at the salon. Sobbing, I told him I was done—I was too exhausted physically and emotionally to keep the salon open. I'd lost control of everything in my life. Our money was all gone, and I had accumulated so much debt. I didn't know how we'd ever get out from under. Most importantly, I'd missed so many years of my life believing that if I just did this one thing, everything would fall into place, and the salon would become profitable. I told Bill I wanted to close the business and go back to being a hairdresser. It was just too hard to keep going at this pace.

This was the darkest time in my life, and it was at that moment that I wanted to give up everything. I was 100% ready to quit. But thankfully, Bill reminded me that we had a vision and a dream to build something special together. Giving up wasn't an option; we just needed to change how we'd been doing things. He reminded me of Einstein's definition of insanity: doing the same thing over and over and expecting a different result. Together that night, we committed to reinventing my salon and getting my life back.

I pledged to stop being reactive and running my life according to other people's version of success with a revitalized passion. I changed how I ran my business, studying how smart business owners, specifically salon owners, had created thriving businesses. I realized what it was to run my business like a CEO for the first time.

This breakthrough changed everything. I relentlessly learned how I could salvage my business, which meant discovering how to become truly profitable. At this point, I didn't have *Profit First* to rely on because Mike hadn't yet published his book. So, I attended every business event I could find. I hired a coach who taught me about the economics of a salon, and we did a complete audit of my numbers. We implemented a cash flow plan that accounted for every dollar spent.

At the same time, I developed my mindset and gained 100% clarity on what I wanted out of life. I shifted my wasted energy to the things that increased true profitability and rebuilt the life I wanted. And you know what? My business started to thrive. That next year we had one of our best years ever. I started taking care of myself and putting myself first, all while nourishing my family and marriage and becoming passionate about my mission—my reason for starting my salon business in the first place.

Once Mike's book hit the streets, I committed to running a *Profit First* salon and implemented every detail in my business. I was able to re-engineer my company and my life completely. It gave me the structure, foundation, and money to repair what had been broken in my salon. It became the operating system for everything I did (and still do) in my business.

Changing YOUR Money Game

Salon owners and independent stylists are great at making money. We love making people feel special and beautiful. No doubt you, dear reader, are the same. And you should feel fantastic about that.

The problem comes from the fact that we're used to exchanging our time for money as a service-based business. Yet, making money in a business is only half the equation. I learned the hard way that the money you make is only worth what your financial model will allow. If you don't have a sound money management system in place, focusing on profits, you will forever live paycheck to paycheck.

Regardless of your vision for your business and life, money is the foundation. We need money to support our mission and the lifestyle we want. To have those things, we don't just need to bring more money in the door—we need to make our businesses profitable.

Most small business owners (salon owners or not) don't truly understand profitability. We're good at making money and spending it but typically don't understand how to save and grow the money we bring in. Spending money without a sound financial model securely in place is a guaranteed path to becoming a Starving Stylist—living paycheck to paycheck, month to month, barely surviving, incurring debt all along the way. The only way to step out of this endless cycle is to make our salons profitable, and that's precisely what we're going to do.

CHAPTER 2

THE CORE PRINCIPLES OF PROFIT FIRST FOR SALONS

"You never change things by fighting the existing reality. To change, build a model that makes the existing model obsolete!" – Dr. Leon Alexander

Before we dig deep into the Profit First methodology, we need to lay the foundation of financial principles. I will explain why much of what you're currently doing with your business finances doesn't work and what to do instead. The first thing we're going to tackle is how we bank as business owners. You may find yourself a little resistant to changing the way you've always done things, but hang in there with me. I promise it's a simple flip in your thinking that will help you massively grow your profits.

Bank Balance Accounting Doesn't Work

I want to introduce an important concept called bank balance accounting. This is how I managed my money for years, and I'm guessing you probably do too. Bank Balance Accounting is simple. It's where you have a single business checking account to collect all your deposits for services and sales in your salon. Then, use that same business checking account to pay all your bills and expenses.

You probably manage your personal checking account like this too because *that's how we're taught to do it*. It's not your fault that you're using this method because *everyone* does. The problem is that bank balance accounting doesn't work if you want a profitable business. This method causes us to make bad spending decisions because the balance you see in your checking account does not give you the whole picture.

Here's what bank balance accounting looks like on a day-to-day basis: We log into our online banking account, look at our balance, and make critical business decisions based upon the current amount of cash sitting in that account, but the *true balance* would factor in the money we owe in expenses and money due. To put a finer point on it, how often have you had a great day of services and sales only to take a look a day or two later and see that you're about to bounce checks or don't have enough in there to cover payroll? Welcome to bank balance accounting.

You can get yourself in a world of hurt by using this system. For example, let's say you check your bank balance, and you are happily surprised to see you have a couple of thousand dollars in there. You decide this is an excellent opportunity to pay for that new line of products you've been wanting or run another ad for a stylist. Maybe you've been waiting for a chance to update some of the equipment in the salon. Since you've got money in the bank, you enthusiastically take the plunge.

Suddenly a new expense comes through that you didn't anticipate, maybe a tax bill. Perhaps you have a plumbing issue that needs immediate attention, or one of your stylists suddenly needs a few days off, and you have to cancel her appointments. So many unpredictable things can bring your checking account balance down to zero, and this is a cycle that repeats over and over again. When your bank balance is up, you feel good and spend money. When the balance is down, you panic and start "robbing Peter to pay Paul."

Traditional Accounting is Destroying Your Business

Since the early 1900s, business owners have been using a traditional accounting system referred to as GAAP or Generally Accepted Accounting Principles. It's still the way accountants are taught to look at your money, and that concept is reflected in all your financial reports. The basic formula goes like this:

Sales - Expenses = *Profits*

If you pull out your income statements right now, you'll notice all your sales and service income is listed at the top of the report. Then you have a *long* list of expenses, and then *way* down at the bottom, you have a single line called Net Profit. This would be any money that is left over after you pay your expenses. If you use accounting software, like QuickBooks or FreshBooks, you are likely familiar with that line.

How often have you looked at your Net Profit at the end of the month only to see a negative number? If you are like me, you've experienced it many times—maybe even every month. You undoubtedly felt like I did—defeated and frustrated when you saw that negative balance because you thought you were doing well that month. You raked in a healthy amount of revenue—even more than usual. But yet again, you can't pay yourself anything that month.

Profit is Not an Event—It's a Habit

Profit First is designed to take the GAAP formula and flip the equation—putting profit before expenses. The formula reads like this:

$$\text{Sales - } \textit{Profit} \text{ = Expenses}$$

The only way to start making consistent profits is to change how you look at numbers. You have to start training yourself to think in terms of *Profit First* before looking at a single expense. This might sound crazy or unrealistic right now, but trust me, that is because the old way of thinking about accounting is all you've been taught. Don't worry! I'm going to guide you step-by-step through the process of changing the way you handle your business finances, and I promise, it's going to be easier than you think.

You've probably heard the famous quote, "Failing to prepare is preparing to fail." This sentiment definitely applies to profits. If you fail to plan for profits, you will not have any profits. The GAAP method suggests you bring money into your business and then pay all your bills before considering or thinking about profits. The problem with this concept is human behavior. We are designed to consume. We've been trained to be consumers our whole life. So, what happens when money comes into the salon? You consume it. You find ways to spend it, and if *you* don't find ways to spend it, *things* will find you. In *Profit First for Salons*, you'll learn a new system to pay yourself first consistently.

Eat Your Veggies First and Other Financial Tips

Mike Michalowicz's book, *Profit First*, introduces four core principles to make your business profitable. To help explain these four principles, Mike compares this system to the actions needed to lose weight. It's the perfect way to describe these principles because it works the same way with your business. As you will see, the concept of losing weight and counting calories is very similar to the actions needed to manage money and control debt.

1. Use Small Plates - When you use a small plate, you naturally eat smaller portions, which means you take in fewer calories. When you take in fewer calories than you normally would, you start to lose weight.

2. Serve Sequentially – When you eat your vegetables first, you change the sequence of your eating patterns. You'll fill up on the healthy food first, and you'll lower your hunger before you get to the rest of the (less-healthy) meal. As a result, you'll automatically eat less, lose weight, and feel better.

3. Remove Temptation – When you want to lose weight and eat healthier, the first thing you're told to do is clean out the pantry and get rid of all the junk food. If those cookies and pretzels are constantly calling to you, it's going to be much easier to lose weight if you're not tempted to grab the snack food every time you feel hungry. Remove the junk food, remove the temptation.

4. Enforce a Rhythm – When you schedule meals every day, you train your body to eat at set times. Consistency is key to a healthy diet, and if you wait until you are hungry to plan out your menu, it's too late. Successful diets include eating at regular, scheduled times and pre-planning your menus.

Let's look at how these core principles apply to business finances.

1. How to Use Smaller Plates in Your Business

The concept of smaller plates is the very basis of the *Profit First* method. It's simple logic that consuming a smaller plate of food will provide fewer calories than a larger plate. That's just common sense. Therefore, we'll take that same thinking and apply it to your money management. Let me explain.

We determined earlier that having one bank account to hold all your income and pay your expenses doesn't work. In the same way you would eat all the food from one large plate, you consume all that money in your single bank account. You'll find a way to spend everything before capturing a single profit. With *Profit First*, we will reduce the size of that spending account and turn it into a "small plate." You will still likely consume the whole plate, but now it's a smaller portion, meaning less money leaving your business. The result will be a bottom line (Net Profit) that is positive rather than negative.

Now, you may think you need all the money in a big account to cover your expenses, so a smaller plate of money won't work. It's natural to think that way, and it may be hard to imagine how you could downsize your expenses right now. But the truth is, your business is telling you that it can't afford all those expenses. Remember, at the core of it, the GAAP method is keeping you in the red. We must change our actions if we want different results.

Using the *Profit First* methodology, you will naturally start creating new habits to "spend from a smaller plate." This new way of managing your cash flow will continually nudge you to question how you consume. You'll start to question the things you've been spending your money on autopilot. You will gradually adopt behaviors that align with your new *Profit First* system.

An excellent way to relate this to hairdressing is to think about your behavior when mixing color. When you open a new tube of color, you give a big healthy squeeze into a bowl. You make a full-color mix to apply a generous application to your client's hair. Just imagine the profits pouring out of that color tube.

Now let's say you barely have an ounce of color left in the tube to service that same client. You can be sure you'll find a way to make that remaining color work. You start thinking creatively. Maybe you don't need to put the color all over the client's head. Possibly, you decide only to put color in the front and adjust enough on the top to make it all look great.

So, instead of costing you $50 for the service, now it only costs you $25. Your profit margin just *doubled*, and your client is thrilled with her hair. She got the same beautiful results without you wasting $25 in color. It takes a bit of a mindset shift to start thinking like this, but it will be worth it because it will help create financial profits *and* happy customers.

2. Serve Money Sequentially in Your Business

If you learn nothing else from this book, you must understand the importance of paying yourself first. We've all heard this wise advice, but even if we try to do it, we quickly go back to paying everything else first. Believe me, I get it. I understand how tough this sounds, but all it takes is a little discipline. Once you see how the *Profit First* system works and how easy it is, you'll be chomping at the bit to put the concept to work for you. Just like eating your veggies first when trying to lose weight, you need to pay yourself first to grow your profitability.

Most business owners fall into the trap of focusing on expenses before profit (GAAP). This trap encourages you to work hard to create sales to pay the expenses to support your sales efforts. Then, before giving profits any thought, you're back into sales mode. It's a never-ending cycle of selling to pay bills. When your focus becomes profitability, that's when the transformation begins. This one mental shift alone will train you to develop a *Profit First* Mindset.

Once that mindset shifts, you will start taking home a paycheck and feeling successful. You'll be motivated to continue acting on the transformative plan. Your excitement will build, and the *Profit First* way of doing things will become your new normal. You'll start sleeping better because you're not worrying about how you're going to make payroll or where you're going to find the money to pay your "already-late" quarterly taxes. You will feel in control of your business. From there, the only way to go is UP. You'll be able to consider how you might grow and scale your business. Now that's a healthy mindset and a healthy business.

The health of your business relies on paying yourself first. It's not a "nice to have" or a luxury. Your business depends on it. Like in everything else, if you take care of yourself first, you can do everything else the right way. Paying yourself first is like putting on your oxygen mask before trying to help another passenger when an emergency occurs on an airplane. By giving oxygen to yourself first, you have the strength and ability to assist others. By paying yourself first, you reduce your stress and worry so you can make wiser business decisions that will benefit your clients and team

3. How to Remove the Temptation in Your Business

I am going to confess something embarrassing to you. My true love in life comes wrapped in foil. When unwrapped, it's a combination of soft marshmallow filling sitting on a sugary round graham cracker and then completely covered in chocolate. It's a delicious dessert called Krembo that I can only get from back home in Israel. Well, let me tell you, when these mouth-watering treats find their way to my house, I can devour a case of them in days. My healthy diet goes right out the window. I tell myself that *I'll be able to control myself and spread out my Krembo feasting this time*, but the temptation always wins. Those yummies are gone before I know what happened, which is why I rarely have them in the house.

This is no different when it comes to money. We are all vulnerable to this same kind of temptation when we have extra cash sitting right there in front of us. When we know we have money in the bank, it's human nature to be tempted to use it for something immediately. And trust me, with your new *Profit First* system, you will start accumulating extra cash almost from day one. Your profit account is going to snowball, which is great! However, since the purpose of building profits is to create consistent long-term wealth, you will move these profits out of sight so that you don't spend your newly saved money on impulse purchases. Be gone, temptation!

4. Enforcing a Rhythm in Your Business

You may have guessed by some of the hints I've been dropping that the *Profit First* method requires you to set up new bank accounts. As we get further into the book, I'll explain everything to you. You will also have a system to determine the proper allocations of money in each of those accounts. Just as you need to plan out your menus when dieting, you'll need to plan where to put your money. Like you need a schedule for your meals when you commit to a diet, you also need a consistent schedule for your money. As part of the overall system, I will teach you how to move your money twice a month between accounts. This method is called the 10/25 rule. If you follow this rule, you'll have a very consistent way to control your entire *Profit First* system.

The 10/25 rule is the glue that holds everything in *Profit First* together. Moreover, it will allow you to run your business pretty much like you do today, only you'll see profits at the end of the month. You will be able to look at your bank accounts and know exactly where you stand, and then get right back to business as usual. This works because you will set a date for all your money exchanges and transfers. It will provide the "rhythm" you need to build your profits and pay your bills.

Wrap Up

With all this talk about changing comfortable habits and monitoring your spending, you may be thinking you'll put down this book and never pick it up again. Please, please don't do that. Anytime we do something outside our comfort zone, even when we really want to change, it feels scary and uncomfortable, but if you keep doing what you're doing now, running your business using the GAAP method, your results are never going to change. You'll be stuck in an endless cycle as a starving stylist living in the burnout zone. I'm offering you a chance to see big, positive numbers under "Net Profit" consistently each month. You just need to be willing to commit to learning and implementing the *Profit First for Salons* solution.

CHAPTER 3

ASSESSING YOUR SALON'S MONEY HEALTH

"The measure of success in business is directly related to the level of profit it achieves."
–Dr. Leon Alexander

My friend and long-time client, Scott Allison, was seriously undercharging for his salon services when we first met. While Scott's salon, The S. Salon & Spa in Fairbanks AK, was a high six-figure business, he could barely pay himself at the end of each month. He was sick of living hand-to-mouth while working 70-hour weeks. So, when he came to me for help, we first evaluated the top three profitability metrics that every salon needs to know—I call them the Big Three.

The Big Three

1. **Time Standards** – the measurement of time that it takes a stylist or technician to complete a service.

2. **Productivity** – the measurement of time that a stylist or technician is booked.

3. **Cost Per Hour (CPH)** – the calculation that shows precisely what one hour costs the business.

It's common in the salon business to hemorrhage profits without understanding where or why it's happening. The first thing we do when we begin working with a new client is to take a close look at their Big Three because we find "bleeds" or money leaks all over the place when we start evaluating a client's profitability. To be truly profitable in your salon's business, you must align your prices with your cost per service and time standards.

Scott's most popular and biggest money-maker was the signature full-foil hair coloring service he and his senior staff members provided to their customers. I suspected he was losing money or at least could have had a more considerable profit margin on the service, and I was right. We discovered the time standards he had allocated for the service weren't accurate. He'd allowed 90-minutes, but his team members were taking two-and-a-half hours to complete the service.

So, what's the problem with that?

Well, to make consistent profits in your salon, you need to know your cost per hour (CPH) for the salon, as well as the *"actual"* time it takes you to perform a service. We'll cover how to calculate your cost per hour (CPH) later in the book, but for now, let's take a look at Scott's results for this service.

Scott's Full-Foil Service

First, we determined that Scott's salon has a cost per hour (CPH) of $60, which means it costs him $60 per hour for his salon to be open. Next, we determined that he was charging $140 for that 90-minute full-foil signature color service. Knowing those two numbers, does that sound like a profitable service? Let's think it through.

Cost per hour x number of hours = service cost

If Scott's CPH is $60, and if the service is 90 minutes, that would be a cost of $90 for that service. The numbers look like this:

$60 cost per hour x 1.5 hours = $90 service cost

By charging $140 for the service with only a $90 service cost, that would mean Scott was making a $50 profit each time the salon provided that service to a client.

$140 charge - $90 service cost = $50 profit

Not too shabby. Not too shabby at all, Scott.

So why was Scott unable to pay himself a salary?

When we analyzed this service, we learned that his team was actually taking two and half hours to complete this service, not 90 minutes. Let's see what happens when we assign the *true service cost* to the equation by changing the allotted time to the *actual time* it takes to perform the service.

Cost per hour x "actual" number of hours = "actual" service cost

We know that Scott's CPH is $60, but if the service is actually taking 2.5 hours, that would mean an "actual" service cost of $150.

$60 cost per hour x 2.5 hours = $150 actual service cost

Since Scott was only charging $140 for the service, but it cost him $150 to perform the service, he was losing money. The salon was "bleeding" $10 each time they performed the treatment. And remember, this was his most popular service, so he was bleeding a lot of profit every single month.

Scott's "Profit First" AHA Moment

When we dug into Scott's services, we uncovered many of these money leaks. It wasn't the case with every service, but enough to make a big impact on his bottom line. These profit holes, though perhaps small, can be the difference between living the life you want and being forced to go deeper into debt each month just to stay afloat.

Scott made a few price corrections and adjusted some time standards, and suddenly the bleeding was lighter. You see, when you start doing this, even a little fine-tuning goes a long way. Those profit adjustments start compounding incrementally, and suddenly you begin to fall in love with the concept of seeing your money grow *without working harder!*

This is exactly what happened with Scott. At first, he was in shock. Then, he fell in love with the idea of evaluating profitability in every nook and cranny of his business. He began applying the idea to every service. It took a little time, but eventually, he experienced a complete mind shift.

He decided that his entire team needed to understand these concepts, so he educated them on his newfound profit mindset. He slowly moved away from doing everything on his own and began delegating profit assignments to key team members. Collectively, they were on a mission to create the cash flow they all desired. Within a year, they had wholly overhauled their profitability, and the results in Scott's business were tremendous.

Scott likes to describe using his new profitability mindset to a system like brushing your teeth—it just becomes something you do without question. It's automatic. Scott went from total frustration to being fully inspired, motivated, and having a highly profitable business in a short amount of time.

An assessment of Scott's business helped him identify his money leaks. And now, along with other changes in his business, Scott only works three days a week behind the chair. He enjoys the remaining days working *on* his business and finally has a real work-life balance to spend more time with his family. He's also achieved several financial goals, including an addition to his house, an investment in a lakeside vacation home, and, most importantly, a chance to give back to our industry and his community. He is proudly living his goals, and like many of our clients, Scott has intentionally created the life he dreamed of when he opened his business.

The Profit First Assessment

Whether your business is simply not as profitable as you would like or is in full cardiac arrest, Scott's story hopefully opened your eyes to the possibilities. Now, you're going to get the chance to start turning your business into a *Profit First* salon.

Remember, *Profit First* is a *cash* management system. We don't do anything on accrual or any funny money stuff. It is straightforward:

Did you get the cash or not?

Did you spend the cash or not?

That's it. Unless cash happens, nothing else really matters, so our focus is exclusively on cash.

YOUR Profit First Instant Assessment

Figure 1 below is the Profit First Instant Assessment Form, and we're going to use it to evaluate your business profitability. It's an opportunity for you, as a business owner, to put the numbers to the test and determine exactly how (un)profitable your business is.

To complete the form, you can write directly in the chart below or you can download a printable copy from the resources section on our website: ProfitFirstSalons.com. That way, you can hang it up somewhere you'll see it daily as a reminder of your profit goals.

What You'll Need

Before we get started, you'll want to gather any reporting you have. If you're currently using accounting software, such as QuickBooks, you'll want to print your *Profit and Loss Statement* and *Balance Sheet*. You'll be able to get most of the numbers you'll need from those reports.

If you have salon software, you can also use that to determine how much revenue you generate monthly, quarterly, and yearly. If you don't have access to these reports, you can estimate based on your knowledge of the business, your sales, and even use bank statements to get pretty darn close.

Ideally, you'll want to have your numbers for the last 12 months. If you don't have access to all of that, or if it feels too overwhelming, it's fine to start with six months or the last quarter. I don't recommend any less because we want to get a range, not just focus on one month. The reason is that the final calculations could be misleading if you had a fantastic month or a rough month.

If your business went through an abnormal period, you should consider not including those months in your Profit First Instant Assessment calculations. For example, if your business was closed for a while, that certainly wouldn't reflect your actual numbers, so you wouldn't want to include those months in your calculations.

All that being said, be as accurate as possible when entering your numbers so you can get a true picture of your profitability and identify precisely where the challenges are so we can address the key problem areas of your business later.

	ACTUAL	TAPS	PF$	THE BLEED	THE FIX
Top Line Revenue	A1				
Material & Subs	A2				
Real Revenue	A3	100%	C3		
Profit	A4	B4	C4	D4	E4
Owner's Pay	A5	B5	C5	D5	E5
Tax	A6	B6	C6	D6	E6
Operating Expenses	A7	B7	C7	D7	E7

FIGURE 1. PROFIT FIRST INSTANT ASSESSMENT

Column A (Actuals)

A1—Top Line Revenue

This number is a complete total of all your sales for the time you are using. You will typically have service and retail sales as a salon or spa. Add them together and put that amount in this cell. Make sure to put in your sales and retail amounts using "after discount" numbers. You should be able to get these numbers straight out of your salon software reports or your Profit & Loss statement.

A2—Materials and Subs

The "materials" we are talking about here are not items such as regular use supplies related to the cost of goods. You will add those types of supplies later in another field. "Materials" in this case means big-ticket items, like construction projects. In the salon world, the materials would likely be zero. Regarding "subs," if your business uses subcontractors to generate 25% or more of your sales, enter the total cost for those subcontractors in this cell. This will be the case if your salon is comprised of suite owners and booth renters that generate most of your income.

If your salon has stylists that are either W2 or 1099 employees, they **do not** qualify as subcontractors. In this case, you would leave this cell as zero.

A3—Real Revenue

To come up with your *real revenue, subtract your materials and subs (cell A2) from your top-line revenue (cell A1).* The number you get when you subtract those two numbers is the actual revenue you generated in your salon for this period.

A4—Profit

Next, in cell A4, you will add any profit you've recognized from the business. This would be money that you have allocated from your salon's earnings into a savings account. You have identified this money purely as profit to the company and that you withdrew as profit only. Chances are, if you're reading this book, you don't have a dedicated profit account. However, you may have a savings account where you sock a little money away. If you do, count that money as profit. If you're doing anything else along those lines where you're moving money into some sort of business savings account, include it here. Put that total number in this cell.

A5—Owner's Pay

This is the money you are paying yourself as an employee of the company. Chances are, you wear many hats and do many different things in your business. You're managing and leading the company, and you need to be paid and paid well for that. If you are paying yourself, put the dollar amount here. Many salon owners are also producers, and they spend hours behind the chair doing client services. If that's the case, add that amount here as well. Total anything you're paying yourself and put that number in cell A5.

Now, this is where it can get a little tricky because we often "pay ourselves" in ways that get categorized under *operating expenses*. For example, you may have a car payment that the company is paying. While it's up to you and your accountant to determine how that works from a tax perspective, the reality is that you are paying yourself that amount if it's a personal car. Therefore, those types of expenses should be counted as income to you.

For example, if you have a $400 monthly car payment you pay out of business funds, that dollar amount goes here. That $400 is considered *owner's pay*. Now, of course, if it's a company car that was purchased *solely* for business reasons and is shared among employees to run errands and other business-related travel, then you could consider that car payment purely as an *operating expense*. But if the car is used for personal and business, it's part of your *owner's pay*.

The same applies to personal life insurance or your monthly cell phone bill. We see a lot of these types of expenses when we evaluate our clients' books. When we discuss this, often salon owners don't view these types of expenses as income to them, but if you really want to evaluate your profitability, you have to accept that these expenses are *the owner's pay because they are for your personal use,* not just the business. Carefully review everything you are currently putting under *operating expenses* to determine if anything should be moved to *owner's pay*.

A6—Taxes

The dollar amount you have saved and already paid towards taxes should be added here. For example, if you have already made a few quarterly tax payments, then total them and add that number here, along with any money you've saved towards upcoming taxes.

If you're like many salon owners, you might not be saving or paying taxes throughout the year. In this case, you are likely using the panic and scramble method, where you leave it all until tax time and then look for some creative way to pay the taxman. If that's the case, place a zero in this cell. And don't feel bad if that's you. I know your stress, and I promise we're going to fix it.

A7—Operating Expenses

Add up all the expenses to run your business and put the total in this cell. If you're looking at your Profit and Loss statement, this will include the "cost of goods sold" *as well as* "general and administrative expenses" categories. Everything you are spending to keep your business running gets added up and put here.

Don't forget to subtract any expenses from those reports that you moved earlier to the *owner's pay*. Back to the example of your car payment, if you moved (added) your monthly $400 personal car payment to the *owner's pay*, then subtract it here from your *operating expenses*. You don't want to account for anything twice.

Great, the hard part is done! Now, double-check everything and make sure that your numbers are correct. Then add up your profit, owner's pay, taxes, and operating expenses to see if the number you get matches your *actual revenue number* in cell A3.

Profit + Owner's Pay + Taxes + Operating Expenses = Real Revenue

If the number you get from adding everything listed above doesn't match your number in cell A3, something's off. Go back and double-check your numbers to get your assessment as accurate as possible. Your *real revenue* needs to match the total of those four cells. We're going to use your *real revenue balance* to get a detailed picture of your profitability, so take your time to get it right.

Column B (TAPS)

Now that we have your *real revenue number*, we're going to move our focus to column B, **TAPS,** which stands for **Target Allocation Percentages.** To determine which TAPS you should use, find the percentages based on your *real revenue range* from the six columns in the chart below (Figure 2: TAPS) and fill in cells B4 through B7 in the

Profit First Instant Assessment Chart (Figure 1) with the corresponding percentages. *These are the target percentages that you'll work towards.* Your starting points will likely be much lower, but keeping these percentages top of mind will help you focus on your goal.

	A	B	C	D	E	F
Real Revenue Range	$0 - $250K	$250K - $500K	$500K - $1M	$1M - $5M	$5M - $10M	$10M - $50M
Real Revenue	100%	100%	100%	100%	100%	100%
Profit	5%	10%	10%	10%	15%	17%
Owner's Pay	50%	30%	15%	10%	5%	3%
Tax	15%	15%	15%	15%	15%	15%
Operating Expenses	30%	45%	60%	65%	65%	65%

**FIGURE 2: TAPS (TARGET ALLOCATION PERCENTAGES)
FOR SALON AND SPA INDUSTRY**

Before we go any further, I want to comment on the target allocation percentages you see in the illustration above. In the original *Profit First* book, Michael Michalowicz and his team evaluated thousands of small businesses across multiple industries to determine the average percentages based on each company's revenue.

While it's a great starting point for general businesses converting to the *Profit First* system, after taking many clients through this process, I've come to realize that some of those percentages in the original book weren't in alignment for salons and spas.

Our industry overall has enormous overhead. Many salon owners have been conditioned to make only modest money in their business and instead rely heavily on the money they make from behind their chairs. We will change that for you with the *Profit First* method, but it's a reality in the salon industry.

For example, a typical salon that runs between $500,000 to $1 million in sales per year runs at 70% to 80% in expenses. These salons are typically paying high commissions to their team, and the owner is often relying on their own service sales to bring any money home for themselves. Other factors include low margins, unprofitable time standards, poor productivity, expensive product lines, and high turnover.

These things are difficult to change and take time. I recognize this, and I don't want to set false expectations. We know that you can't just change the commission structure for your whole team and swap out your product lines overnight. This would result in chaos in your business, and you would lose staff and clients. I want this to work within the structure that you have right now.

Based on all of this, and for this assessment exercise, I have found it better to work with what we have in place right now since we're not going to change things overnight. So, the percentages in the table above are adjusted to fit today's typical salon and spa business.

Now, I want you to move forward with the self-assessment and get a sense of where your business stands as it relates to similar-sized salons and spas.

- **Column A:** When a company is doing less than $250,000 in revenue, it's typically one employee. Maybe you're a solopreneur in a suite or booth rental situation. If so, you're likely doing $250,000 per year or less and would fall into this category.

- **Column B:** This is your typical small salon with three or four chairs and doing between $250,000 to $500,000 per year. Owners in this category are doing much of the production from behind the chair. This was me for many years as the top producer in my small salon. We see a lot of clients at this level who want to learn how to grow and scale to the next level.

- **Column C:** When a salon is making $500,000 to $1 million per year, you might have a team of five or more, and the company is no longer solely dependent on your service production. We see businesses here struggling with high expenses and very little meaningful profit.

- **Column D:** Salons making above $1 million and under $5 million per year are bigger salons. Often, they have two or three locations or high square footage and 20 or more stylists. Once you're at this level, you need a whole new type of strategy for your business. You've grown significantly and are likely working only on your business, not in it. This is where we focus on larger projects and transformation to increase your profitability.

- **Column E:** These salons are making $5 million to $10 million and are small chains of salons where the founder is out of the day-to-day operations and working on the growth and vision of the company.

- **Column F:** These are your ten million to $50 million businesses. Once you've achieved this, there are many ways that we can continue to maximize profitability. These are often salons that are national or even global.

Once you identify where you fall in terms of *real revenue range*, add your Target Allocation Percentages (TAPS) into each cell.

For example, if you are a Tier 2 salon (column B) with $250,000 to $500,000 in yearly sales, you would put 10% for profit, 30% for owner's pay, 15% for tax, and 45% for operating expenses.

Column C - Profit First Numbers (PF$)

Going back to our Profit First Instant Assessment chart (Figure 1), the next column shows the actual dollar amounts you should allot to each row. *To get the numbers for Column C, multiply your TAPS by your real revenue number.*

For example, if your real revenue number is $600,000, your numbers would be:

Profit PF$ = 10% = $60,000
Owner's Pay PF$ = 15% = $90,000
Tax PF$ = 15% =$90,000
Operating PF$ = 60% = $360,000

Don't worry if you aren't hitting these numbers yet! That's why you are reading this book—learning exactly how to reach those goals. I'll teach you some strategies to do just that in the next chapter. For now, we just need to focus on figuring out where you are now, so we know what you need to do to get where you want. You'll be working towards these target numbers and percentages incrementally.

Column D - "The Bleed"

This column will indicate the health and profitability of your business based on if you are allocating less or more to each category than you should be to reach maximum profitability.

To figure out this number, *subtract your profit first $ from your actual number* to see where you stand at this point.

Going back to our example, if you should be allocating $60,000 for profit but you've only allocated $35,000, then your "bleed" is minus $25,000. This means you will need to grow your profit by $25,000 in the period you are reviewing.

To determine your numbers for each column:

> **Profit**—Subtract C4 from A4
> **Owner's Pay**—Subtract C5 from A5
> **Taxes**—Subtract C6 from A6
> **Operating Expenses**—Subtract C7 from A7

Column E "The Fix"

The final column just requires one word: increase or decrease. That's "the fix"—should you increase or decrease the amount of money you put into each "bucket," *profit, owner's pay, tax, and operating expenses.*

Examples of The Profit First Instant Assessment

The Profit First Instant Assessment is a snapshot of your profitability. We see a lot of different things when we do this with clients. For example, you might find that you're paying yourself too much, which is why you're running up debt and struggling. Below you'll see what that situation would look like on the Assessment.

	ACTUAL	TAPS	PF$	THE BLEED	THE FIX
Top Line Revenue	A1 357,900				
Material & Subs	A2 0				
Real Revenue	A3 357,900	100%	C3 357,900		
Profit	A4 0	B4 10%	C4 35,790	D4 -35,790	E4 Increase
Owner's Pay	A5 132,540	B5 30%	C5 107,370	D5 25,170	E5 Decrease
Tax	A6 0	B6 15%	C6 53,685	D6 -53,685	E6 Increase
Operating Expenses	A7 225,360	B7 45%	C7 161,055	D7 64,305	E7 Decrease

FIGURE 3. PROFIT FIRST INSTANT ASSESSMENT EXAMPLE 1

Or, you might find that your expenses are suffocating you. When you consistently have operating expenses that are nearly the same as your revenue, you're literally going to be bringing home no money. You're working for free. Unfortunately, both of these scenarios are very common in the salon industry. These are two of the most common issues we see with our clients.

		ACTUAL	TAPS	PF$	THE BLEED	THE FIX
Top Line Revenue	A1	692,520				
Material & Subs	A2	0				
Real Revenue	A3	692,520	100%	C3 692,520		
Profit	A4	7,500	B4 10%	C4 69,252	D4 -61,752	E4 Increase
Owner's Pay	A5	64,879	B5 15%	C5 103,878	D5 -38,999	E5 Increase
Tax	A6	12,335	B6 15%	C6 103,878	D6 -91,543	E6 Increase
Operating Expenses	A7	607,806	B7 60%	C7 415,512	D7 192,294	E7 Decrease

FIGURE 4. PROFIT FIRST INSTANT ASSESSMENT EXAMPLE 2

You've probably had a sense already of where you stand, but now the numbers are telling the true story for sure—no more guessing. You will see where to make changes to start moving the needle in the right direction, regardless of how small the incremental changes are. What matters is that you know what direction to go in for each area of your Profit First Assessment.

Next Steps

This whole chapter has been one big step, so the homework assignment is to complete your Profit First Instant Assessment and get those numbers as accurate as possible.

This will be a major reality check for you, but knowing the actual numbers will trigger a desire to step up and take action today. This can be a painful process because the truth of the matter is most salon owners do not run their business profitably. They're incurring debt and struggling paycheck to paycheck just trying to survive. This assessment will be your starting point to make a change and start turning the ship around.

Final Thoughts and Tips

If you don't have QuickBooks or any other accounting software and are struggling to come up with these numbers, it's a clear sign that it's time to delegate the management of your books to a professional. I would encourage you to hire a bookkeeper (and accountant) who are familiar with *Profit First*. If you need help with this, you can find more information on our resources page at ProfitFirstSalons.com.

At this point, you may be feeling overwhelmed or bad about what your assessment is telling you. Perhaps you believe you've failed as a business owner or that you've just made one wrong decision after the next. Maybe you're exhausted and feel like giving up.

If any of that describes how you feel, I want you to stop, take a deep breath, and understand one essential thing: You are 100% normal. We have all been there. Every successful business owner has been down this road at one point or another. It's part of the process, and it doesn't matter how long you've been stuck.

What matters is that you recognize where you are and that it's time to make a change. This is part of the transformation. This is how it works. It's just a matter of time that your business will turn around and thrive if you commit and follow the *Profit First* methodology. You'll start looking at everything with a completely new set of eyes. It's exciting. It's almost like starting your business all over again.

It's my privilege to be a part of your journey. I honor you and your commitment, and I genuinely want this change for you, your family, and your team. Stay determined, stay focused, and keep going. You've done the hard work already, and now we're going to put the pieces in place, one by one, and rebuild together.

CHAPTER 4

SALON MONEY: THE FUNDAMENTALS

"If no mistake have you made, yet losing you are
...a different game you should play"
– Yoda

By now, I hope you realize the importance of having Profit First implemented in your business. Simply put, Profit First is the number one, most essential thing you need to build a sustainable salon business. Fortune 500 companies have been using this method for years, so why shouldn't we? But while all successful businesses must rely on sound money management, the lifeblood of any business comes from sales and income. Whether you sell products or services, you can't function without revenue inflow.

Moreover, having a profitable income is what you really need. Therefore, this book wouldn't be complete without talking about revenue. Before we go any further, I want to share a strong belief that we engrain in our clients.

> *"The key to transforming your salon into an automated money-making machine has NOTHING to do with your business model, your systems, your advertising, or your staff.*
>
> *But it has EVERYTHING to do with understanding your numbers."*

Let me say that again—*The key to transforming your salon into an automated money-making machine has EVERYTHING to do with understanding your numbers.*

Here's the thing, most of us have a hard time when it comes to understanding numbers for different reasons. Maybe math class was always challenging for you, or it's always been a challenge for you to grasp the concept of numbers. Whatever the reason, you don't need to worry about it anymore because I will help you understand your numbers like a pro. I will show you what the numbers mean and which ones you need to understand to grow your salon's revenue.

I love this chapter because once I understood which numbers were vital in my business, there was no limit to where I could take my company. I want the same feeling for you. I want you to understand precisely the key drivers and the numbers that will allow you to gain that momentum without everything falling on your shoulders. Knowing your numbers is true freedom.

According to the market research done by industry leaders, most salon and spa owners don't understand their potential growth, and most salon owners are not making money from their business. Even though they work full days, day in and day out, they're still living paycheck to paycheck, and many owners are working behind the chair 80% of the time. The only take-home money that "owner/operators" make usually comes from providing services to their clients. It's impossible to grow your salon this way, so I'm going to teach you the numbers that will allow you to set goals for your entire business and team so you can grow your salon and spa *without depending on your income from behind the chair.*

THE BENCHMARKS

Let's start by looking at the benchmark metrics for a profitable salon in Figure 5 below. These are the key percentages you can reach to maintain your financial goals. I'll explain what each benchmark is as we go.

THE BENCHMARK NUMBERS

85%	60%	85%
Retention of Base Clients	Retention of New Clients	Productivity (Hours Sold)

FIGURE 5: THE BENCHMARKS

Base Retention

The first benchmark is an 85% retention rate of your base clients. We define a base client as any regular customer that has been to your salon for at least three visits. To create consistency in your cash flow, you need to be retaining 85% of these clients. Successful salon and spa owners are in that zone. If you're at 75% retention, then you are just getting by. If you're at 65% retention or less, then you're losing money and making clients unhappy, or both.

New Client Retention

The next benchmark you want to achieve is 60% retention of new clients. That means that 60% of the new clients who come to your salon need to be coming back for more. Most salons I see are at the 30% and 40% mark, which means they're working like crazy, constantly trying to get new clients. They're running on a hamster wheel. They're practically losing those new clients as they come through the door.

Productivity

Finally, you need to reach 85% productivity in your salon. This means 85% of the hours available are booked with services. And these need to be true, productive, income-earning hours. Maintaining 85% productivity is where you need to be to have that absolute freedom I know you're looking for.

Let's take a look at how to calculate productivity. You'll see this illustrated in Figure 6 below.

CALCULATING PRODUCTIVITY	
Total Hours Sold ÷ Total Hours Available **= Productivity**	**EXAMPLE:** 200 Hours Sold ÷ 400 Hours Available **= 50% Productivity**

FIGURE 6: CALCULATING PRODUCTIVITY

To work out your current productivity percentage, first calculate all the hours you are open for sale. This would be all the hours available for stylists to be booked.

If you have 10 stylists and each works 40 hours a week, you have 400 hours to sell per week. Now, if you take all these available hours for sale and compare that to how many hours you sold, that's your productivity percentage.

For example, if you had 400 *hours for sale* and had sold 200 hours of those hours, you would divide 200 by 400 to get 50% productivity.

This means your team has only been busy 50% of the time they are available. You have at least another 35% to increase your productivity to hit the 85% benchmark. Your productivity percentage is the number one key driver to understanding how much more potential you have to grow in your salon.

It is essential to know every month because productivity is always where you need to increase. If you are at 50% productivity and increase it to 60%, it will hugely impact your revenue. You can do it step-by-step. Even if you increase it by 1% every month, you will be generating more income each step along the way. You should always work towards the 85% target and keep your productivity high. This is where the profitable salons operate.

High productivity brings other great benefits like a reduced turnover in staff, advanced training, and improved consistency during slow months, etc. When the salon is busier, it creates more energy and better momentum with your team. In addition, a bustling salon will have a buzz about it which will attract more clients and newer stylists who will be eager to work there.

Profit Per Hour

The following significant number is your *profit per hour*, illustrated in Figure 7 below. This is something you must know in your salon if you truly want to understand your numbers, and more importantly, your profitability. Knowing your *profit per hour* will allow you to make critical business decisions to meet your profit goals. For example, it can help you align profitable prices with your services.

FIGURE 7: PROFIT PER HOUR

I often start by asking salon owners what their *profit per hour* is, and 99% of the time, they have no idea. If that is you, don't worry; we'll go through this one step at a time. To calculate your *profit per hour*, you will need to figure out your *income per hour* and your *cost per hour*. To make it work for you, you have to know all three of these numbers, so I will show you how to do these calculations.

Step 1:

First, you'll calculate your *income per hour*. Take your total sales for the month—all the service and retail sales. Then take the total sales and divide by the number of *hours sold* for the month. This will give you your *income per hour*.

Total sales ÷ Hours sold = Income per hour

Step 2:

Next, you'll need to calculate your *cost per hour*. Start by totaling your monthly expenses, including *payroll, general expenses, cost of goods sold,* and *owner's pay*. Make sure not to overlook any expenses to get precise, accurate numbers. Now, take your *total expenses* for the month and divide them by the *number of hours sold*. This will give you your *cost per hour*.

Total expenses ÷ Number of hours sold = Cost per hour

Step 3:

Perfect, now we can calculate your *profit per hour*. You'll take your *income per hour*, less your *cost per hour*, and then you'll have your actual *profit per hour*.

Income per hour – Cost per hour = Profit per hour

Let's look at some examples of calculating your profit per hour.

PROFIT PER HOUR EXAMPLE

Total Sales & Services for the Month: $40,000
÷ Total Hours Booked for the Month: 200 hours
= Income Per Hour ($200 per hour)

Total Expenses for the month: $30,000
÷ Total Hours Booked for the Month: 200 hours
= Cost Per Hour ($150 per hour)

$50 Profit Per Hour

FIGURE 8: PROFIT PER HOUR EXAMPLE 1

In example 1 above (Figure 8), your *total sales* come to $40,000 a month, and you divide that by 200 *booked hours* for the month. That means that your total *income per hour* is $200 per hour.

Next, if you have $30,000 in *total expenses* for the month and divide by those same 200 *hours booked,* that means that your *cost per hour* is $150.

So now, if you take the $200 *income per hour*, minus the $150 *cost per hour*, you're left with $50 *profit per hour,* right?

It would be incredible to have a $50 profit per hour! Unfortunately, that's not very realistic. Our industry target is to be at 20% profit per hour. That would be 20% of your income going to profit. Using our example of 20% *profit* on $200 *income per hour* would give you $40 *profit per hour.* I'll take that any day of the week.

When we do this with new clients, I often see total expenses matching their income per hour. In the following example, Figure 9, Example 2, you can see the numbers for yourself—when your *total expenses* equal your *income*, you're making zero profit. Not a good place to be.

PROFIT PER HOUR EXAMPLE

Total Sales & Services for the Month: $40,000
÷ Total Hours Booked for the Month: 200 hours
= Income Per Hour ($200 per hour)

Total Expenses for the Month: $40,000
÷ Total Hours Booked for the Month: 200 hours
= Cost Per Hour ($200 per hour)

$0 Profit Per Hour

FIGURE 9: PROFIT PER HOUR EXAMPLE 2

Sometimes, new clients come to us in even a worse situation. We often see the following scenario: *cost per hour* is $250, and their *income per hour* is only $200. They are running in the negative. They're bleeding money. (Remember "The Bleed" column from your Profit First Instant Assessment?) Look at Figure 10, Example 3, to see the breakdown.

PROFIT PER HOUR EXAMPLE

Total Sales & Services for the Month: $40,000

÷ Total Hours Booked for the Month: 200 hours

= Income Per Hour ($200 per hour)

Total Expenses for the Month: $50,000

÷ Total Hours Booked for the Month: 200 hours

= Cost Per Hour ($250 per hour)

-$50 Profit Per Hour

FIGURE 10: PROFIT PER HOUR EXAMPLE 3

If reading this makes your palms sweat and your hands tremble, you can rest assured that what comes next will give you the confidence to make the necessary changes to turn around your salon's profitability. Remember, I just explained that it is common for our clients to come in barely breaking even or losing money. Don't be alarmed if that's what your numbers are telling you. You aren't alone. This is what I do every day—help salon and spa owners make their businesses profitable *no matter where they start*. Next, we're going to discuss some ways to make positive changes in your business starting today.

How to Increase Your Profits

Once you've figured out your current *income per hour, cost per hour, and profit per hour*, you can immediately start to make adjustments to improve your profits. Here's a shortlist of some of the best and most popular ways you can make your salon more profitable:

- Adjust Your Pricing

- Improve Your Time Standards
- Lower Your Expenses
- Increase Retail Sales
- Raise Your Productivity

While we work on all these areas with our clients, I'm going to focus on three of the most significant areas that can make the quickest impact on your business—adjusting prices, improving your time standards, and lowering your expenses.

Adjust Your Pricing

When salon owners start to think about whether they are charging enough money per service, they typically have no idea what to base it on. I will ask an owner how they came up with their charges for services, and they rarely base their rates on their *profit per hour*. It's more likely that they just called around to find out the going rate of other salons in their area and then decided to charge either $5 more or $5 less. If that's you, then you're imitating prices somebody else is imitating from somebody else and so on and so on. A salon can't be profitable using this pricing model. Luckily, this is an easy fix now that you know your numbers.

To know exactly what to charge, you need to know your actual *cost per hour*, and then you need to determine the amount of *profit per hour* you want to make on that service. Only then can you know exactly what you need to charge for each service. This is one of the first things we fix with our clients. We help find their accurate numbers and align their service rates with their profit goals. Isn't this awesome? Beyond awesome! Now you're taking charge of your business in a whole new way.

Cost per hour + Desired profit per hour = Price for service

Earlier I told you that our industry targets 20% profit per hour, so that's a great number to shoot for when you consider what you want to tack on to your cost per hour to come up with your pricing. If you're not there yet, don't worry. Once you figure your hourly numbers out, you can improve them immediately by rethinking your pricing and applying a slight increase.

If you're afraid to do it, which many people are, take it slow. You don't have to increase the prices of all your services at once. Put a plan in place to incrementally get there over time. Take it one step at a time. I will tell you that implementing this strategy is the quickest way to boost your salon income immediately.

When I first learned that I could intentionally change my prices and create the profit I wanted, I became obsessed with the idea of rebuilding my entire menu of services. Suddenly, I had clarity when it came to setting my prices. The first thing I did was analyze my color services. I quickly realized that we were following a boring, common trend by offering very plain options to our clients. We had three simple color services, which were:

- one-process
- hairline color service
- full foil application

We simply called them full foil, hairline color, and one-process – clearly not one of my most creative moments when I came up with those names. On top of that, after going through the cost-per-hour analysis, I quickly determined that these services were extremely unprofitable.

I decided to completely re-brand all these services into a complete color maintenance program. I trained my staff to introduce it to every client who came into the salon for color. We would sit with the client during our consultation and completely map out their subsequent three or four visits. We renamed the three services Level 1, 2, and 3 and explained how each level served a specific purpose. Then, we would use a combination of these three levels to build a custom color plan specifically for them.

By offering our service as a color maintenance program, we achieved every client's long-term goal with their hair color. We would map out a plan for their next three or four visits, including two or three consecutive Level 1 services and then a full foil Level 3 service. This pre-planned maintenance program sky-rocketed our pre-booking numbers and created a whole new level of professionalism within our team.

Our clients loved it because they were getting a highly customized program that was perfectly aligned with their hair color goals, and more importantly, we gave them a solution to fit their budget. Over time, clients became so familiar with their custom program they would speak to our staff using the same terminology that we were using on the floor. They knew exactly when they were due for a Level 1, 2, or 3, and they were always excited to be part of the process.

Rebranding our color services into a structured maintenance program allowed us to align our pricing to match our profit goals easily. For example, our one-process service was $45 for a 30-minute application before changing things. Once we rebranded to our color maintenance program, that same service (now called Level 1) went to $95 for a 30-minute application. That simple service quickly became our highest profit margin service. It took a junior colorist 30 minutes to apply a color and glaze and provided our salon with a 170% profit margin for that service!

Here is a step-by-step breakdown on determining the profitability of that service:

- First, we determined the cost of that service. At the time, we had a salon service cost of $70 per hour. So, a 30-minute service would have a cost of $35.

- Next, we subtracted the service cost ($35) from the price to the client ($95). The difference gives us a profit of $60.

Price ($95) - Cost ($35) = $60 Profit

That's a $60 profit for a $95 service. We created a 170% profit margin on a basic color service. It was terrific, and our clients never questioned the price simply because it had been presented as part of an overall solution. As time went on, we became known as the color gurus in our area. Our staff blossomed and became highly motivated. The whole team was completely aligned with our new direction. This process transformed my company overnight, and it all started by knowing my cost per hour and the profitability for each service.

Improve Your Time Standards

The next thing we consider is whether you are using the appropriate time standards. Remember Scott? He is now living his dream life, and it all started when we took a cold, hard look at his salon's time standards.

What if you have a service that takes an hour to complete? Ask yourself how you could adjust that one hour to 45 minutes instead. If you could just change that one-hour service to a 45- minute one, you would immediately create more profit for yourself—without working more hours.

This was the situation our client Lyndsey was in when we met her. She was charging $200 for a one-hour facial. Since her cost per hour was $195, her profit per hour was only $5. No wonder she was barely making ends meet. It was a rare treat when she brought home a paycheck at the end of the month.

After finding her benchmark numbers, we recommended reducing the time she allowed for a facial from one hour to 45-minutes. Immediately, her profit margin improved. Then we took it a step further. We asked her what type of service she could offer during those 15 minutes she just saved. As a massage therapist and an aesthetician, she decided to start offering a 15-minute chair massage at the end of the facial to raise her profit even more.

Suppose the client didn't want a chair massage—no problem. She spent that extra time educating her clients on products that would benefit their skin based on what she'd noticed during the facial. She tracked this strategy over the next few months, and to her surprise, she sold an average of two products to clients during those 15 minutes she'd salvaged.

So now, Lyndsey is making more income, more profit, and her clients are thrilled with the service they receive. Now that's what I call a win-win! And that's just one of many ways we were able to improve Lyndsey's time standards.

Cut Your Expenses

As hard as it may seem, whenever I work with a salon or spa owner, we always find unnecessary costs to cut out from their monthly expenses. Believe me, you have money bleeding from your business. I want you to find that money as fast as possible. It's easy to convince yourself that you *desperately need* everything listed on your expenses, but I'm telling you, it's there. You just have to know where to look.

You can do many things in your salon and spa business to find the bleed, and we will do a deep dive on cost-cutting later in this book. For now,

I want you to use that profit mindset we've been working on and find 10%. Here's how you'll do it.

Calculate all your recurring expenses over 12 months. We've made it easy to do by creating a spreadsheet for you. You can download it at ProfitFirstSalons.com. Not a fan of spreadsheets? Instead, you can simply download all your credit card and bank statements and highlight all recurring expenses for the last three months. This list should include your rent, subscriptions, utilities, internet, training costs, online classes, magazines, etc. All recurring expenses need to go on this list.

Now don't freak out, but you're going to cut 10% off this list, and if you are freaking out, don't feel bad because you're not alone. Our clients consistently say the same thing when we do this with them: "Impossible." Well, sorry (not sorry), that word is not in our *Profit First* vocabulary. You can delete that word right now because I have not had a client yet who hasn't successfully cut 10% off their expense list.

First, highlight everything *not* directly tied to running your business efficiently and retaining clients. In the beginning, it may appear that you need everything, but you have to take your time and drill down on each of these. Any subscription that will not stop you from doing business needs to go now. Even if it's as small as a $10 per month expense, these types of charges will add up quickly.

Next, you're going to negotiate pricing with every single vendor expense that you're keeping. Start with rent since that's your biggest expense and one that you can try to lower by speaking with your landlord. Now more than ever, landlords are working with their tenants to help keep them stay up and running. In 2020, with the pandemic and the shutdowns we went through, our clients were able to lower their rents significantly. Most landlords didn't want them to go out of business, and they were willing to adjust (or restructure) rents as a result. It might take a little creativity, but it's worth it. Lower rent can be a massive game-changer for your business.

Remember the old saying that everything is negotiable? Well, that is true, and it's time to start. Identify your expenses, begin by cutting the ones that are not directly impacting your bottom line, and negotiate everything else. Don't stop until you have found 10%.

Wrap Up

We discussed a lot of big topics in this chapter, so let's review what we just covered.

The key benchmarks and target calculations that will give you immediate growth in your revenue and profits are:

Base Retention—Target at 85%

New Client Retention—Target at 60%

Productivity—Target at 85%

These benchmarks work together to increase revenue and profit. Your productivity increases immediately when you raise your base and/or new client retention percentages.

Next Steps

- Calculate your *income per hour* and your *cost per hour*.

- Figure out your current *profit per hour* and where it needs to be so you can start operating like a profitable business. At that point, start identifying the key things you can adjust to make the extra profit you need.

- Evaluate whether you're setting prices that are aligned with your profit goals.

- Find ways to improve your time standards that will create the added space and time on the schedule needed to help increase your profits per hour?

- Find ways to cut your expenses by up to 10% on items that won't impact your ability to serve your clients or run your business efficiently.

- Determine what strategies you can put into place to increase productivity.

- Know these numbers for your business and *track them monthly*.

- Calculate and track monthly:

  - Number of hours sold

  - Total expenses

  - Income per hour

  - Cost per hour

  - Profit per hour

Remember what I said at the beginning of this chapter: The key to transforming your salon into an automated money-making machine has NOTHING to do with your business model, systems, advertising, or staff. It has EVERYTHING to do with knowing and understanding these numbers. This one area of focus was a complete game-changer for me in my salon, and it will be a game-changer for you too… I promise!

CHAPTER 5

SETTING UP PROFIT FIRST FOR YOUR SALON BUSINESS

"A Jedi must have the deepest commitment,
the most serious mind." – Yoda

When Anna Walsh approached me for the first time, she was in the process of opening her new salon, Lola Hair Studio, in Cambridge, MA. Over the past year, she'd been working full-time as a stylist and manager in a commission salon in preparation for transitioning into salon ownership. With this experience, Anna felt comfortable knowing the requirements of running a salon.

Like so many salon owners, this is the typical path towards going on your own. I always see it with high achievers who constantly look for the next step in their personal and professional growth. In Anna's case, the culture at the salon she was working for was not doing it for her anymore. She wanted her own salon so she could have more freedom and money so she could build her legacy. We talked for a while about her exciting journey and decided she should reach back out to me after she was up and running.

Exactly one year later, I got a call from Anna. She had launched her hair studio and hired a team. They had five chairs in full operation. Anna was working full-time behind the chair, and she felt she was well established in her new place. I congratulated her on the success—it was a big deal that she'd come so far in only a year. But Anna didn't feel that same enthusiasm. We spoke for a while and quickly determined what I see often; Anna lacked clarity in her salon's vision.

Anna knew she wanted success, but she couldn't identify what success looked like for her. She didn't truly understand what it takes to feel successful. When she had opened her salon, she had believed she knew exactly how to run the business, but just one year in, she realized that she needed a guide to help her build a profitable foundation.

I give Anna so much credit for that decision. It often takes salon owners far too long to reach out and finally get help. I can tell you it took me several years of struggling before I hired my first coach, and I could have avoided a lot of debt and frustration if I'd acted sooner.

When the two of us started our work together, Anna quickly confessed that she didn't know how to read her numbers. In fact, she really didn't understand her numbers at all, but Anna knew that if she got a good handle on them, she'd be able to grow and do so much more with her team. Until then, she lived like so many salon owners—barely making it month to month while working full-time behind the chair.

Once we got started, my first step was to introduce the concept of running a *Profit First* Salon. When I explained the *Profit First* formula (Sales

- *Profits* = Expenses), she saw the logic right away and started organizing her thoughts and ideas in terms of profit. Everything came into focus for Anna, and she put complete faith in the *Profit First* way. Anna immediately adopted and applied the concept of the five foundational accounts (which we'll discuss next). By diligently implementing *Profit First* in her business, she completely removed fear from the equation. Now she knew exactly where she was and where she was headed. Money started building and piling up in her profit account.

By adopting a *Profit First* mindset, Anna took her salon to 35% profitability in only her second year in business. And for the past three years, Anna has continued running her business with yearly profits exceeding 20%. Moreover, during the 2020 COVID-19 pandemic, she maintained the salon's profitability and kept her entire team intact. Not only did she endure that challenging year, but she also managed to pay herself each month, stay current with taxes, and build her profit account.

None of this would have been possible without her *Profit First* system. She followed the formula and stayed dedicated to the results. It was easy for her to stay on track because the system was already working. She didn't have to think about where to allocate the money. She paid the company first and then paid herself. After that, everything else just naturally fell into place.

Anna loves being a hairdresser more than she loves building systems, but she definitely loved building her profit system because it's simple and delivers immediate results.

Turn Accounting on Its Head

We already spoke about the way entrepreneurs typically manage cash flow. By default, we all use a cash management system based on one primary checking account. It's a system called Bank Balance Accounting, and it's designed to lose us money. Having one bank account to manage all your income and expenses, along with payroll, taxes, and emergency funds is destined to fail. This is because we've gotten in the habit of checking our online bank account to see how funds are looking and then making business decisions based on that balance. But as you know, the number we see on the screen is not the actual balance. It's not reflective of your true, actual cash flow because the balance hasn't been adjusted for profits, owner's pay, and taxes yet.

As you'll see, when you set up the *Profit First* system, you're going to hack how you check your account by tweaking a few things to ensure you're making wise business decisions. This is the magic of *Profit First*— it's designed to work the way YOU work. *Profit First* is not going to ask you to stop checking your account daily and making decisions, but instead is going to give you a system that ensures that you will see your real balance whenever you check it.

The difference is that your account funds will already be adjusted for profits, owner's pay, and taxes. This new system will allow you to do things the way you've always done them but with the confidence that your balance is accurate. So, let's dive in and take a look at how to make this happen.

The Five Foundational Accounts

Until now, we've talked about the concepts and reasons why we're making these changes in the first place. You've worked out your benchmark numbers and have decided on strategies that will raise your productivity and profit. Now it's time to get started making those changes.

The steps we're about to go through are the foundation of the *Profit First* system. This will help you build the framework of everything you'll do in your business from now on. Initially, it may seem a little awkward, but I promise this will be a game-changer in your wealth-building journey.

First, we will say good riddance to Bank Balance Accounting and the GAAP cash management method. In its place, you're going to set up five checking accounts at your primary bank. You want them to be checking accounts rather than savings accounts because they'll be easier to manage, and you'll have more flexibility. You will set each of them up so that you'll have access to all of them through an online banking portal.

Profit First - Five Accounts

1. INCOME – the account where all your deposits go

2. PROFIT – the account where you take your profit before everything else

3. OWNERS' PAY – the account where you pay yourself for working in the business

4. TAX – the account where you set money aside for taxes

5. OPEX – the account for all remaining money that you'll use for expenses (OPEX stands for operating expenses)

Profit First - Two "No-Temptation" Accounts

The idea behind these two accounts is to put the money you set aside for profit and taxes in a place where it's not easy to get to, thereby removing the temptation to dip into it. We all know how easy it is to "borrow" a little here and a little there. Before you know it, all the money you've put aside for a rainy day (or taxes) is gone. You need to start thinking about your profits and taxes as non-negotiable. These funds are untouchable.

Remember, we're building a habit, and by accumulating profits, you'll be on the path to building wealth and having freedom in your life. No more sleepless nights worrying about how you're going to pay your taxes this quarter. That's a terrible place to be—I know; I've been there—and I promise you, this system will fix that problem once and for all!

Once you have your five foundational accounts set up with your primary bank, the next step will be to set up two more bank accounts. These two accounts will be used for profit and taxes. I know this might seem a little redundant, but you're going to be accumulating money in your PROFIT and TAX accounts, and we need to get that money out of sight. The best way to do that is to set up two duplicate accounts, called PROFIT HOLD and TAX HOLD, in a secondary bank. You're going to regularly transfer the money from your PROFIT and TAX accounts from your primary bank to these two accounts.

Now, your "no temptation" accounts should be set up as savings accounts. They will accumulate money over time, and therefore, we want you to collect interest on that money while it's there. Once the accounts are set up, you'll need to link these accounts to your primary bank so that you're able to transfer money from your primary bank's PROFIT and TAX accounts. This might take a couple of days, but once it's set up, you'll be able to transfer money from one bank to the other quickly.

Set Your CAPS

To get your whole *Profit First* system started, you have to choose how much you want to commit to allocating right now in each of the five primary accounts. This is the amount you are willing to take from each sale to allocate to your four allocation accounts. These percentages will be your CAPS—**Current Allocation Percentages**.

We've already discussed TAPS--**Target Allocation Percentages**, at length earlier. And while TAPS is the goal—the percentage where you'll end up after you've turned your salon into a fully-fledged *Profit First* business, your CAPS is the percentage you begin with today. You will begin allocating a percentage of every sale to each of your new *Profit First* accounts from this point forward. I cannot stress enough how important it is to start with a very manageable number. Don't go overboard. It's much more important to start with a percentage you know you can handle. The last thing we want is for you to allocate too much and then have to go back and pull money from your profit account. Remember, no more borrowing from Peter to pay Paul.

We have started some clients with CAPS at 1% profit, 3% owner's comp, and 1% tax. Often, our new clients are making no money from their salons, so we have to start by assigning a tiny allocation percentage so they can get a taste of what it's like actually to pay themselves. Remember, this is a starting point, and it's better to start with *something* rather than not start at all, so even an allocation as small as this will be a win.

A Quick Review of TAPS

In chapter 2, where we did your Salon Profit Assessment, I had you use the allocations that I've tested specifically for the salon industry. We recognize that our industry is unique when it comes to operating expenses. With the high cost of staff commissions, training, education, high-end products, maintenance, utilities, etc., we realize that operating expenses need to be realistic when setting up our Target Allocation Percentages (TAPS).

Therefore, I encourage you to use this table when picking out your targets because it's much more in line with what we see across our industry. I also want you to recognize all these numbers as guidelines. When you initially set up your allocations, make sure to put a little time and thought into what makes sense for you. Crunch your numbers, and come up with realistic targets.

	A	B	C	D	E	F
Real Revenue Range	$0 - $250K	$250K - $500K	$500K - $1M	$1M - $5M	$5M - $10M	$10M - $50M
Real Revenue	100%	100%	100%	100%	100%	100%
Profit	5%	10%	10%	10%	15%	17%
Owner's Pay	50%	30%	15%	10%	5%	3%
Tax	15%	15%	15%	15%	15%	15%
Operating Expenses	30%	45%	60%	65%	65%	65%

FIGURE 11. TARGET ALLOCATION PERCENTAGES (TAPS)

Make sure to push yourself and work towards percentages that are a little out of your comfort zone, but don't make them so high that you feel it's hopeless and completely unattainable. Your goal should be to reach your TAPS percentage over the next year or two, depending on where you start. You're not trying to get there in a month. The goal is to create a road map to build a long-lasting, sustainable business.

Set Up Your Accounts

As we prepare to set up your new bank accounts, we must discuss how you should name them, so there's no confusion later.

Now, when I say to name your accounts, I literally want you to set up the nicknames in each account. For the most part, any online banking portal will allow you to assign a nickname to your bank accounts. There is a precise way you need to name these within your bank portal.

Here's how to name them:

First, determine your CAPS for each account-- the percentage of the amount you decide you're going to contribute with each deposit.

For example, if you decide that you're going to allocate 3% of every sale to your profit account, add "3%" after the word "Profit."

After that, add the Target Allocation Percentage in parentheses. Write in the abbreviation "TAP" and then the percentage. Do this for all four of your allocation accounts.

Your nicknames would look like the example below (but with your own allocation percentages).

PROFIT 3% (TAP 10%)

OWNER'S COMP 5% (TAP 15%)

TAX 5% (TAP 15%)

OPEX 87% (TAP 60%)

Picking the Right Banks

Our clients are often told by their bank that they need to carry a minimum balance in each account. Some banks will tell you they won't allow you to have multiple free checking accounts. We have found that if you explain what you're trying to do and that it's non-negotiable, most local banks want to keep your business and will make it work. If they don't, it's time to start interviewing new banks. Credit unions work out great in many cases, as they are often flexible and more willing to work with local businesses.

It may take a little effort on your part to find the right bank, but in the end, it's going to be worth it to have all these accounts set up with no minimums. You don't want to be worrying about keeping a certain balance when you're making transfers. The idea is for this to be quick and easy. You'll see just how easy in an upcoming chapter when we give you details on how and when to transfer money between accounts. It should take you a minute or two for all your allocations. To see a list of our top referred banks, go to ProfitFirstSalons.com

Inform the Troops

Let your bookkeeper and accountant know what you're doing. They need to be on board with these changes. They need to be happy and willing to work with you. The last thing you need is to have them push back because they feel your new money management system isn't necessary or creates extra work for them. We've heard this from many clients, and it's usually just a matter of educating them on your goals. Don't worry. For now, let's get things set up with the banks first, but keep it in mind, you need your financial team fully on board with your *Profit First* system. If needed, you can always check our resources page, ProfitFirstSalons.com, for information on how to find bookkeepers and accountants that work with *Profit First*.

Final Thoughts

You probably have at least one checking account already that you're using in your primary bank. That account can be used for your OPEX account. Since you're likely paying bills from that account already, it's a good one to use for expenses. Then just set up all the new accounts to reflect your INCOME, PROFIT, OWNER'S PAY, and TAX accounts.

Next Steps

STEP 1: Set up the four additional foundational accounts in your primary bank (The fifth one will be your current checking account, which will be used for operating expenses.) Remember to make these "checking" accounts and set them up for online banking. Call them INCOME, PROFIT, OWNER'S PAY, and TAX. Add the nickname "OPEX" to your current account.

STEP 2: Set up your two "no-temptation" accounts with another bank as "savings" accounts so you can earn interest as you accumulate funds. Call them PROFIT HOLD and TAX HOLD accounts. Don't request online portal access to your "no-temptation" accounts. The idea is to set it and forget it. Once you transfer money out from your PROFIT and TAX accounts in your primary bank, you don't want to have online access to that money. Again, that money will accumulate, and you'll use it in the future for the right reasons.

CHAPTER 6

RUNNING A PROFIT FIRST SALON

"Sales are flattery, profit is sanity" – Dr. Leon Alexander

Amy Roland of A. Roland Salon in New Cumberland, PA, was one of our first Salon Cadence clients. She was perfect for our program because her goals were aligned with all the things we focused on. She was tired, overworked, and anxious to build a business that served her lifestyle. She was tired of working behind the chair five days a week and having the company rely so heavily on her personal production. She knew she wanted to build systems to streamline each area of the business. She wanted a team that she could empower to run those systems. Her branding was outdated, and she wanted a whole fresh new look on her website and throughout the salon.

More than anything, Amy wanted to be profitable. She was so tired of working endless hours to make so little money. She loves her business and wanted everything right, but she was losing hope. Like so many salon owners, she had resigned herself to the idea that she was never meant to have great financial success in her life. It seemed impossible to her that she could have complete control while growing her wealth and enjoying time freedom.

When I met Amy, she was already aware of these things, but even more so, she understood many of the actions needed to make those changes. I asked Amy what was holding her back and stopping her from getting started. As so often happens, Amy broke down in tears. She said that she was afraid of making any changes. Her money situation was always so tricky. She would live paycheck-to-paycheck and often couldn't draw an owner's salary. For years she had wanted to expand and make the company work for her, but year after year, she was always afraid to invest the time and money for what she needed to do. She was stuck in the woods and afraid to get started, and it was too hard for her to take that initial step.

Knowing this, we decided to start with baby steps. We built a road map that involved minimal but highly strategic action items. We quickly implemented *Profit First*, but we kept the allocations to a manageable percentage. What happened was magical. With each passing day, Amy picked up momentum. Each small step compounded into larger successes. It didn't take long before the company started to see a significant change.

The team began feeling the energy, and a new culture developed that supported the growth and the vision Amy had for the business. Amy's salon was going through a major transformation without even realizing it. Every day, she became better and better at growing and implementing her strategy. She started believing that her company was profitable, and for the first time, she made it to 18% owner's income.

Amy is still a client and continues to fine-tune and run *Profit First* in her business. She constantly strives and pushes for new goals and results year after year. Even through COVID-19, Amy was able to maintain her profitability. She completely changed her money story, and she did it by taking manageable steps.

The point of the story and this whole chapter is that even the most meaningful goals can be accomplished through a simple, basic strategy. As you're about to see, we will set some goals in this chapter that will initially seem out of reach, but we'll do it in a way that won't feel overwhelming. I'm going to show you how to set this up so that you'll barely notice any changes, and just like Amy, you will have a major shift bubbling right at the core of your business. Are you ready? Let's do this.

The Formula

It all starts with the basic formula: **Sales - Profit = Expenses**. From now on, this is your new mantra in the business. It's time to ingrain this formula into your brain and fully commit to your new way of life! Just like Gee, Scott, Anna, and Amy, you need to wake up every day with your Profit First mindset ready to go.

Share It with the World

Nothing will help you commit to this journey more than sharing it with your team, family, and friends. In addition, you want to share it with your extended team, including your banker, accountant, bookkeeper, financial advisor, etc. Anyone who is part of your salon journey needs to know that you are now a *Profit First* business. Wear this mantra on your sleeve like a badge of honor. Let them know that you're on a mission to build profitability and excellence in your company. There's nothing that can help reinforce your mission and build momentum more than getting the support of those around you.

Make Your First Allocation

Now, since you're using your old primary checking account for OPEX, you should have money in there already. Your first step is to make sure that you leave enough money in that account to cover any outstanding checks for payments that have already been scheduled. You want to ensure those payments are covered.

For example, let's say you currently have $5,000 in that account, and you know you have $3,000 in outstanding checks and expenses already committed. In that case, leave $3,000 in there and use the remaining $2,000 to make your first allocation.

Next, I want you to transfer that remaining amount ($2,000 in our example) from the OPEX account into the INCOME account. This will be the starting balance for your new *Profit First* system! Going forward, you're going to be depositing every dollar earned from your salon services and retail into your INCOME account. Only use the INCOME account for deposits, nothing else.

If your salon software system makes bank deposits directly from credit card payments, make sure those deposits go to your INCOME account. Also, when you physically go to the bank and manually deposit checks and cash, put everything in the INCOME account. Setting up the INCOME account for all your deposits is essential to ensure the system works correctly. From that INCOME account, we will be transferring money to the other four accounts regularly.

From this point forward, you will start allocating all your income to the remaining four allocation accounts according to the CAP percentages you decided to start with. Remember, the CAPS are the starting percentages, and your TAPS are the targets you will grow to over time.

If we stay with the example above, we will allocate that entire $2,000. Using the percentages in our earlier example, you would send 3% to PROFIT, 5% to OWNER'S COMP, 3% to TAXES, and 87% to OPEX. Doing the math, that would be $60 to PROFIT, $100 to OWNER'S COMP, $60 to TAXES, and the remaining $1,740 to your OPEX account.

Now, this is extremely important, so I want you to read this and promise you will do this - ALWAYS make your allocations in the exact order we just used in the example above. *Allocate your PROFIT First.* Then Owner's Pay, Taxes, and lastly to OPEX. It's part of the profit mindset we are building. You must always think about profit before everything else, with expenses at the end. Remember the formula: **Sales - Profits = Expenses**.

You are ready to make your first allocation using your actual numbers. Allocate everything in your INCOME account. Use the percentages you decided to start with, and once completed, you're done. Simple as that. Congratulations, you've made your first allocation!

Get Your Rhythm (the 10/25 rule)

Now that you have the system set up and ready for allocations, I want to talk to you about getting in a rhythm. Remember when we went through the core principles of *Profit First*? The fourth core principle was Enforce a Rhythm. We talked about dieting and learned it's well-known that eating your meals at predetermined, scheduled intervals is the most efficient way to burn calories and speed up your metabolism.

With *Profit First* money management, it's no different. We need a rhythm. In our coaching business, Salon Cadence, we focus on building a rhythm for everything we do. That's where the "Cadence" comes in. Cadence is a consistent rhythm design to optimize your actions. Once you have a system in place, the most crucial step is to put it on autopilot. You want to teach your team to have a strong process and schedule for all your systems. This is how you can build a finely tuned machine related to running your business, and having this will allow you to focus your energy on running the company like a pro.

Setting a rhythm to your allocations is pretty simple. You will use the 10th and 25th of each month as your allocation days. These are the two days of the month when you will allocate all the money built up in your INCOME account and transfer your CAP percentages to the other four accounts.

We have found that the 10th and 25th of each month work perfectly. They align with most of the bills that you pay throughout the month. Typically, you pay rent on the first of the month, and many of the subscriptions come later in the month. By doing things this way, you're spreading out your allocations so that, ideally, the money you need to pay your bills is always there in your OPEX account.

Now, in the first few months of running your *Profit First* system, it's fine if you want to make weekly allocations to get the hang of it. In fact, it's a good idea to allocate more often as you start building this new habit, but over time, you should fall into the twice a month (the 10th & 25th) pattern.

Don't Forget Your Two No-Temptation Accounts

Your PROFIT HOLD and TAX HOLD or "no-temptation" accounts will get your profit and tax money out of sight, so you don't cheat and borrow from these accounts. You will transfer the entire balance out of your primary PROFIT and TAX accounts into your secondary bank PROFIT HOLD and TAX HOLD accounts on the 10th and the 25th, along with your other allocations. Frequently the transfer between your primary and secondary bank will take a few days to complete, so you will likely see your profit and tax allocations sitting in the primary bank for a day or two, and then you'll see a zero balance in those two once the external transfer hits.

Owner/Operator Pay

If you are like many salon owners, you still perform client services and are likely in the habit of paying yourself based on the money you generate from your clients. If this is the case, I want you to do two things:

First, make sure you're paying yourself as a technician right along with your other staff when you do payroll. Next, you need to start paying yourself a wage as a manager. How you do this will depend on your accounting, so you should discuss this with your accountant. But no matter how you set it up, you should get in the habit of paying yourself something as a manager for running your business. If you're not performing services, you will only pay yourself as a manager.

Doing this will make it much easier for you to budget and manage your Owner's Pay instead of simply taking money out of the business as you need it. Those forms of payments show up randomly on your balance sheet as distributions, which can be confusing. We find that our clients get into their rhythm and spend less when they have a consistent method of paying themselves because they have a predictable budget. Remember, you should always pay yourself first–allocate your income before paying any other bills.

YOUR QUARTERLY MILESTONES

Each quarter throughout the year provides an opportunity to true-up and reward yourself for the money you are saving and the great job you're doing as a business owner. These are huge milestones in the *Profit First* system, so let's go through them one at a time.

Quarterly Profit Distribution

This is when you get rewarded for being a wise and profitable business owner. All your hard work and hours building a business and managing a team should come with a reward, and this is it.

You will take a profit distribution from your PROFIT HOLD account every quarter. Use the first day of each quarter to take a distribution. On the 1st of January, April, July, and October, go to your PROFIT HOLD account in your "no-temptation" bank and pay yourself 50% of whatever is in your PROFIT HOLD account. This is your reward for running your business profitably!

Now listen closely. This is your money to spend on YOU. This is not money to go back into the business. You need to honor that "profit mindset" you've been developing, and that includes creating a habit of looking forward to this distribution.

This should not be used to pay bills in your business. That defeats the whole purpose. The idea is that you've already cut costs, and this profit allocation represents the actual profit from your business. It may be small in the beginning stage, but it's going to get substantial over time. We currently have clients that take 20% profit allocations on every penny they earn in their business. Imagine how much that adds up. When they get their 50% quarterly distribution, we're talking about some serious cashola!

Do something fun with this money, or put it towards something important to you and your family. Promise me that you will reward yourself properly and not use your quarterly distribution to catch up on bills in your business. Take your profit every quarter, and use it for your own purposes. This is celebration time!

Pay Those Taxes with Confidence

The next thing you'll do each quarter is pay the government. This is where you're going to make your quarterly tax payments based on the estimates you receive from your accountant. I can't tell you how many clients come to us initially and are not making these quarterly payments. They don't have that profit mindset and instead dump all their cash flow into expenses, convincing themselves they can't do it any other way.

Well, those days are gone for you, my friend. You are now a *Profit First* Salon and paying taxes on time is part of the system. You're going to be making that tax payment on time every quarter. Just like you took your profit distribution, you will also pay the taxman.

Ultimately, you'll want to be allocating enough in taxes to cover your quarterly estimates. However, I realize that in the beginning, you likely won't have the total amount sitting there in your TAX HOLD account. But, given that you are probably not allocating anything towards this currently, it's better to get started with something. Remember, we're building a habit, so whatever you have allocated and sitting in your TAX HOLD account is a win.

Get with your accountant to determine your quarterly tax payment and pay it with the money in your TAX HOLD account. If the balance doesn't cover the full amount of the payment (yet), you'll have to get that money elsewhere, just like you've been doing it all along, but having at least a little money in your TAX HOLD account will reduce some of the pain you feel when paying your estimates.

Adjust Your CAPS

One last action to take on your Quarterly Milestones is to adjust your CAPS. Every quarter, I want you to move your percentages a little closer to the actual Target Allocation Percentage (TAPS). Even if you only started with 1% towards profit, it's ok to take baby steps. Each quarter try to move it up by one more percentage, or more if you can, but keep it within reason. Only bump it if you're able to commit.

Don't forget to bump your taxes allocation as well. If you are not already hitting your tax estimate, this is another percentage you want to increase over time. The goal is to reach 100% of your quarterly tax payment. Stick with it, and you'll get there, I promise.

You'll have spectacular momentum going, so work the system to your benefit. Don't make your allocation percentages so high that you get to the point of stressing out on every distribution. Push yourself just enough so that you're chipping away and getting closer to your goal by building more and more momentum each quarter.

Year One Milestones

When all is said and done, you're going to look back and realize your first year flew by, and you've become a real pro at your *Profit First* system. By now, your current allocation percentages (CAPS) are growing and moving in the right direction. You've taken quarterly distributions where you rewarded yourself with actual profits in your business. You've saved money towards your quarterly tax estimates, so you've reduced the anxiety that comes with making those payments.

You have been taking 50% distributions from your PROFIT HOLD account each quarter, which means you will undoubtedly have money building up from the other 50% that you haven't touched. In Mike Michalowicz's book, he calls this your rainy-day fund. This money is for you to decide how you want to use it. It's precisely what a rainy-day fund should be—money that can go back into the business for growth, or you can use it for unforeseen circumstances, expansion, training, education, etc. You can also choose to leave it there and let it continue to grow. We have clients accumulating enormous sums of money in their PROFIT HOLD account. One client has over $50,000 in that account and is saving towards a commercial property for her salon.

Yes, by now, you will have created the best habit that any business owner could wish for—you're using *Profit First* to build a new way of life.

CHAPTER 7

CRUSH YOUR
DEBT FOR GOOD

"It's not the daily increase but daily decrease.
Hack away at the unessential." – Bruce Lee

COVID-19 came out of nowhere, it seems. Atlanta was locked down for two straight months. When it was time to go back to the salon, Kalena Duru, owner of KBB Salons in Marietta GA, didn't want to go back. She was exhausted. Before the lockdown, she had 15 employees. After the lockdown, only one stayed with her. She became depressed and went into hiding. Her anxiety became so intense that her blood pressure elevated to an alarming height. She found herself home, unable to function, and did not want to get out of bed.

Thankfully, something switched in her brain. Something switched in her mindset that helped her dig deep inside and realize she had to fight through this challenge. Maybe it was me calling her every day, kicking her in the ass to get out of bed. Maybe it was just pure guts and determination to fight through her fears, but something switched.

Knowing Kalena the way I do, I believe it was pure instinct we all possess at the deepest levels, something inside that refuses to give up. The day you decide that you're going to control your life and not become a bystander. You're simply not going to let external circumstances control your actions. That moment when you decide this is your time to *reinvent, reimagine, and redesign your life intentionally.*

What would you do if you suddenly lost everything? It has certainly happened to many people, and maybe it's happened to you already. What would you do? Would you stop living? Of course not. You would take everything you know and all you have learned, and with every bit of strength in your bones, you would start again. Because that's what we do. We are warriors. Well, there's no difference right now. Let's start again, begin again.

Kalena got up, went back into her salon with her one devoted team member, and started over. She had Salon Cadence to help and coach her back, but it was her powerful mindset that set the course. She recommitted to knowing and understanding every number in her business. She redefined her values and her purpose. Ultimately, she completely changed her thinking and belief system and applied a renewed purpose in everything she did from that moment forward.

Fast forward 10 months to the time I am writing this, and Kalena just bought her first home, a long-time goal of hers. She went from the one employee who stayed with her to hiring and developing six new team members who believed in her vision and shared the same goals, mission, and beliefs. She has accumulated money in her profit account. She completely updated her systems to provide freedom and flexibility in her life. Was it easy? No, she suffered like nothing else, but she's a true warrior, a Jedi, and now she's working on the next level because she can. Because she has the profit to do it, she's implementing precisely what the *Profit First* system suggests.

Debt is the Killer of Dreams

I started this chapter off with the story of Kalena and her triumphant return back from a terrible and hopeless time in her life. The pandemic was a sudden event that knocked her into dire circumstances overnight. And just like the pandemic turned Kalena's business upside down, I believe that debt is the single biggest source of destruction in most salon businesses. The difference is that debt is a quiet killer in your company. It feeds on your profitability without you realizing what's actually happening.

Accumulating debt is usually something that occurs quietly and slowly over time. It's like a hidden disease spreading throughout your business, wreaking havoc each step of the way. Debt camouflages itself and tricks you into thinking you're doing so much better than you really are. It gives you a false sense of security and allows you to operate on a foundation that's built on thin ice. When I think about debt, I picture a sinister villain lurking around every corner, looking for any possible way to sabotage your business.

When we look at our numbers and see that we've had a great month in total sales, we immediately feel good and celebrate our accomplishment. We constantly check to see if revenue was higher than in previous months. We tend to refer to these as the best months we've ever had and create this fictitious notion that we're doing great, but the reality is that we're one lousy month from completely running out of cash. One high revenue month does not reflect 12 months of increased debt. Let's face it, if you had a month with a positive cash flow of $12,000 but you have over $12,000 in credit cards, how financially stable is the business really?

In that scenario, you'd have no profit in the business. Many clients come to us with stories of incurred debt and some arrangement with the bank to pay them back over time. Here's the major problem with this. You believe you're going to make payments and pay off the debt entirely over the agreed-upon time. However, you don't change how you're financially managing the business. So, what happens? Your spending habits don't change, and you continue to add to the debt.

How often have you made arrangements with one credit card, only to start using another credit card for new expenses? Not to mention, the arrangements you get from credit cards are criminal. One of our clients had so much debt accumulated that she had an agreement with her lender to pay "interest-only" at 21% interest. How can you ever pay that off? Meanwhile, she used another credit card to pay for things she clearly couldn't afford.

When you start doing these things, you are digging a nearly impossible hole to get out of and essentially putting your business on life support. The bottom line is this: **If you need to incur debt to run your business, then your business is telling you that you can't afford those things you are charging in the first place**.

Please read that last sentence again and keep reading it until it sinks into your soul. It's a very logical concept, but most of us don't want to hear it and prefer to turn a blind eye. Instead, we convince ourselves that we just need one more month to get by before we figure things out, but that day never comes.

Unfortunately, too many business owners learn this the hard way and only start to take corrective action after it's too late. One of our salon clients suffered in this *debt chaos* for years. Her business was well established and produced over $1 million in yearly sales. From the outside, it would seem like she had a successful business, but in reality, she was surviving on credit cards and building debt every month. It was an agonizing way to live, and she suffered greatly as a result. The banks finally decided to cancel her ability to use any of her credit lines at all. She suddenly could not rely on her credit cards, and her entire business went into a downward spiral, literally overnight. Sadly, she was never able to recover and had to close her business. This is what can happen if you play that game.

How to Get Started on your Debtless Journey

Right from the very beginning of my salon ownership journey, I believed that to be successful, I had to grow the business as fast as possible. I was committed to the notion that you have to spend money to make money. I adopted the philosophy that the more money I spent, the bigger I could get and the more successful I would become. Nothing can illustrate how damaging these beliefs are more than my decision to open a spa.

At the time, I had a tiny little hair salon, about 600 square feet, with four stations, two sinks, and a tiny color room. Perfect for me to learn the business, take my time and develop my artistry. But since I was all about growth, I started hiring people on day one of opening my salon. It didn't matter their level of experience. If they wanted to work, I wanted them. Before I knew it, I had a small team, and I was on my way to building my business. Lucky for me, Bill had an excellent job, so I didn't have to worry about cash flow. I could just focus on growth and expansion.

Less than a year into owning my new salon, I had the brilliant idea that adding a spa to my business should be the next step in building my empire. A small two-room office space right above my salon had just become vacant. It was perfect. I could have a waiting area with one massage room, one room for facials, and a little area for doing pedicures. Oh, my imagination ran wild with this idea. This was going to be the start of my thriving salon and spa enterprise. Just what I needed to really take off.

When we consulted our accountant Dave, he and Bill spent the entire meeting trying to convince me that opening a spa was a bad idea. They wanted me to slow down and learn how to run a successful (and profitable) hair salon before venturing out to something new. They wanted me to focus on little things, you know, like getting all my stations completely booked, learning how to manage a team, and operating while turning a profit. You know, silly things like bringing home some money before taking on something new.

But I wouldn't budge. I was committed to growth—to making headlines and competing with the big "successful" salons and spas. After all, they didn't know my business like I did. My clients loved me and wanted to see me conquer the world. I had my new team, and I was sure they would be there for me. I was on a mission and didn't need to hear about taking things slow. I finally convinced Bill that all I needed was to borrow a little more money from our savings. I would open this spa and pay us back in no time.

The spa's grand opening was epic. I had news channels, belly dancers, fancy food, and hundreds of people showed up. There wasn't enough room in the parking lot or my salon to hold everybody. I just knew I'd been proved right—the spa was a brilliant idea.

I'd put a ton of time into planning my event and naturally had picked out the most luxurious lines to carry so I would have everything on full display. I went with the most expensive spa treatment line I could find, a line four to five times more expensive than anything else out there. That, I decided, would show everyone how upscale we were. I wanted to cater to the people that had money. That's how I was going to make it big. My theory of growing fast and spending money to make money was going to get me everything I'd dreamed of…and quickly.

That spa became my *Field of Dreams*. That voice in my head was me, speaking loud and clear, "Build it, and they will come." I put my heart and soul into that spa, and for a short time, it made me happy. But unlike Kevin Costner and the magic of Hollywood, I was playing with real money and real-life circumstances.

My new venture soon went from my exciting pet project to my new money pit. I knew nothing about turning a profit in my salon, let alone a spa. Suddenly, I worked like a madwoman, splitting my time between the salon and spa. I ran up and down those stairs 200 times a day, hiring, firing, training new staff, ordering supplies, managing clients, tracking sales, and on and on, but no matter how hard I tried, the business was bleeding money.

My dreams were big, my vision was endless, and my debt grew like weeds. Yes, we brought clients through the door and put money in the register, but at the end of the day, I was barely able to pay my employees or rent on time. I started robbing Peter to Paul, and it didn't take long before my stress and anxiety consumed me. My *Field of Dreams* had become a nightmare. I did everything I could to make it work. After one full year in operation, I knew that my spa had no chance, not while I was still trying to figure out my hair salon business. I did the only thing I could do. I closed my spa for good.

It was a one-year project that cost a ton of money and created a lot of debt, which took me years to dig myself out from. That was a challenging period, but I realize it was an essential lesson in my journey as I look back now. It gave me the clarity to see that only focusing on growth can destroy your business. If it's not done strategically, with profitability, it doesn't work.

As I've learned later in my business life through *Profit First*, building your business on a smaller scale, focusing on profitability, can create much more wealth in a shorter amount of time than my old "grow fast, spend fast" philosophy. Your bank account will flourish if you combine profitability with being incredibly good at what you do. Take it from me, this isn't the movies. This is business. It's the real deal, and luckily there is a recipe for success.

Debt-Crushing Strategies

Here are a few time-tested strategies to help you begin to crush debt. These tips are by no means an exhaustive list, nor are they intended to replace the advice you may get from a licensed accountant. However, once you stop paying for things on credit and pay yourself first, all these strategies are fair game. Use them all, and you'll start chipping away at that debt for good.

1. The first thing to get your debt under control is negotiating with all of your lenders. Ask them to give you the lowest interest rate possible. Additionally, maybe they can freeze your account for a few months. We all know that that's what happened during COVID-19—many lenders froze accounts for a few months and didn't charge interest. That tells us that they can do that. Make a list of your creditors and work your way down the list,

negotiating with them all—bank, credit card companies, private lenders, you name it.

2. Create a new allocation bank account called DEBT. Hopefully, your new *Profit First* mindset has already come up with that idea by now. If you have debt, your allocation accounts will become INCOME, PROFIT, OWNER'S PAY, TAX, DEBT, and OPEX. Notice where DEBT is located in the sequence. Build it into your system as the second to last allocation. Then, negotiate like crazy with those lenders so you can realistically pay them down and run a profitable business.

3. Stop using borrowed money. Cut your expenses to where you can operate without any form of debt. Go back to Chapter 4 and become obsessed with the section on cutting expenses. If you have a lot of debt, bump your cuts up to 15%, 18%, or even 20%. Take no prisoners. You need to get to this now and be relentless. Many companies have done this successfully and completely turned around their businesses, while just as many salon owners have stuck their heads in the sand and slowly faded away. Let's make sure you fall into the first category and get back on track.

4. When you have enormous debt, whether credit cards, personal debts, banks, or private investors, you need to apply the same concepts you've been learning throughout this book. Whether you have $12,000 in debt or $400,000, you still need to start every day by committing to the *Profit First* system and setting up your allocations. Always pay your PROFIT, OWNER'S PAY & TAXES first. Then, and only then, start paying down your debt.

5. Use the leftover 50% after your Quarterly Distribution to pay off debt. So, keep 50% for yourself and pay 50% towards your

debt. Remember, after each quarter you will be taking your profit distribution of 50% from the PROFIT HOLD account. While you have debt, rather than saving money for a large purchase or a rainy day, put that remaining 50% to the best use by paying down your debt with it.

6. In some cases, you could use a portion of the 50% Quarterly Distribution that you pay yourself to pay down your debt faster. However, this is in extreme situations. The ONLY time you should use some of your personal 50% *profit distribution* for something other than to treat yourself is when it is going toward accumulated debt. And please, ONLY do this if you have stopped using debt to run your business. Use just a portion of your PROFIT HOLD because you still need to reward yourself. Even if you only give yourself a 10% profit distribution each quarter to reward yourself with a pizza and a movie, take it and enjoy. You deserve it. Then use the other 40% to pay off debt until it's gone forever.

7. Start by paying off your smallest debt amount first, and then the next smallest debt until you have all of them paid off. It's easiest to pay off the credit cards with the smallest balance first, and it will give you a quick, satisfying win. Don't worry about getting the highest interest rate cards paid off first. Just get that first one done. For example, if you have three credit cards with $1,000 on one, $5,000 on another, and $12,000 on the last one, start by knocking off that $1,000 card. Getting one card paid off quickly will motivate you to continue to crush your debt. As Mike would say, "Wealth is an emotional game, and we want you to learn how to fall in love with saving more than spending."

8. Fall in love with saving. There is no better feeling as a business owner than when you get rid of wasteful expenses—when you find and fix the bleeding profit. Cutting unnecessary expenses offers you an immediate boost to your bottom line. Start by downloading 12 months of bank statements and going through them line by line, searching for the bleeding areas you can plug right away. Maybe you're subscribing to iTunes or some old subscription you don't use. Cut them now. Even if it's $10 here, $15 there, you'll find a hundred dollars you can save each month before you know it, and that's a huge difference. I promise you that you won't miss them. Knowing that money is set aside for something intentional feels way better than spending money on something wasteful and unnecessary.

9. The next thing you probably want to think about is cutting back on things you outsource, like advertising, marketing, social media, etc. Do you really need to have them right now? My guess is that it's more important for you to create cash flow. You don't have to cut them forever, but right now, you need to focus on getting control of your debt rather than growing your business—which is likely to mean accruing even more debt.

I'm sure you feel resistance around this and maybe don't believe what I'm telling you. Let me give you an example to show you that I know what I'm talking about. My coaching client, Patrick, had been spending over $2,500 per month on marketing—website development, SEO traffic, etc. While marketing is important, we discovered that his new client retention was only 17%. That means that all the money and time he was spending to acquire new clients was blowing right out the door. We cut this expense out until we could figure out why his new client retention rate was so low. Once we knew that, we could fix the bleed and then resume his marketing activities when he could see a real return on his investment.

So, if you are spending money on marketing, such as Yelp or Google ads, collect the data to see if you are getting 3x the return on your investment. If you put $1 into ads and get $3 or more back, you are getting the kind of return that can really grow your revenue. If this isn't the case, cut this expense and find something that will give you a better ROI. If you aren't measuring these statistics, you can't possibly know if you are making a wise investment with your marketing dollar or not.

10. Do you have a credit card with tons of mystery subscriptions on them that pop up randomly? We've all built up subscriptions that renew yearly, and we forget about them because we're not even using them. If your credit card is filled with this stuff, just cancel your credit card. There, problem solved.

11. Be mindful of accumulating bills for the sake of earning SkyMiles or points for various company perks. I see many people hyped about earning these points, but they have to spend money to get them. Many people who are hooked on gaining points spend more than they normally would, just because they think they will gain extra benefits from spending. If you're defeating the purpose, then what's the point? I suggest holding off on purchasing until you have the money allocated for it in your budget.

If you have a lot of debt to crush and you're barely making any money right now, don't stress out about the long journey to get there. Believe me, I know that's easier said than done, but chunking down your debt and focusing on paying off that next loan will keep you motivated to spend less and save more. Just remember to keep your eyes on the target, and it will happen. Take small steps, and you will see results. Remind yourself of this every day.

Hopefully, these tips will get you started towards eliminating your debt. Remember, we are on a mission to set up your business for profitability. Accumulating debt is the complete opposite of that goal. Practice your profit mindset every day by avoiding running your business on debt.

CHAPTER 8

BOOKKEEPING FOR PROFIT

"Knowing is not enough, we must apply.
Willing is not enough, we must do."
– Bruce Lee

For some reason, entrepreneurs have no problem jumping "all in" to create products and services, marketing plans, sales strategies, etc. It must have something to do with our creative DNA and powerful vision. On the one hand, that's a good thing because it is the fuel that keeps us going. On the other hand, these things alone will rarely make us financially secure.

By now, you understand that profits and good money management are usually just an afterthought for entrepreneurs. Profits are left to chance, and we find ourselves tossed and turned in heavy rapids without a paddle before long. This is often the case with our new Salon Cadence clients.

They're moving fast but completely out of control. So, the first thing we need to do is create some profit-building momentum.

As you've probably experienced in other areas of your life, it is not easy to break old habits. Like all entrepreneurs, salon owners are pretty consistent when doing the things that feel natural to us, but we fail miserably at those uncomfortable things like getting our numbers and finances in tip-top shape. If I could point to one thing that helps our clients begin to turn things around completely, it's when we introduce them to Tiffany. Hopefully, you have your own Tiffany already, but chances are you don't, and even if you do, she is likely not doing the things you need.

So, who is Tiffany? She is the ultimate *Profit First* bookkeeper—probably the most important person you can enlist in your *Profit First* journey. She is the one who stands between your entrepreneurial dreams and your financial report card, the person who monitors and tracks your financial activities and then presents them back in a crystal clear and concise way that tells you the complete story about the health of your business, in a way that allows you to make powerful business decisions that will positively impact your bottom line.

Out of the thousands of coaching sessions I've done over the years, none are more satisfying than my *Salon Owner Bookkeeping Session*. This is where I introduce our new Salon Cadence clients to Tiffany Gregory, our resident *Profit First for Salons* bookkeeper. She runs a bookkeeping company that focuses on building profits in every aspect of your salon and spa.

Most salon owners have some sort of bookkeeping software like QuickBooks or FreshBooks, but no matter how excellent your software is, it can only spit out accurate reports if you are entering the correct data. So often, we find incomplete or inaccurate data entries when we first look at our new clients' books. Making decisions based on the wrong information is a massive problem. When your data is incorrect, you'll inadvertently make bad choices and end up hurting your business more than helping, so let's fix that right now and get you the right reports with the correct data.

Profit & Loss Report (a.k.a. The P & L)

Nothing can get you up to speed on your salon's profitability more than a clean Profit & Loss report (P & L). This is one of the most important ways to analyze your business. The purpose of the P & L is to give you a snapshot of your income and expenses over any given period. Many salon owners who have bookkeeping software (like QuickBooks) already know how to pull a P & L. But to tell you the truth, most of them have no idea what numbers are the most important to pay attention to. Moreover, they rarely use the P & L to make their business more profitable by cutting back on all the extra stuff they don't need.

PROFIT AND LOSS
March - April, 2021

	TOTAL
Income	
Membership Income	5 618,00
Retail Income	15 270,01
Service Income	67 193,58
Total Income	**$88 081,59**
Cost of Goods Sold	
Backbar - COGS	3 189,06
Merchant Processing Fees	1 978,88
Retail - COGS	635,50
Service Payroll - COGS	33 009,48
Total Cost of Goods Sold	**$43 812,92**
Gross Profit	**$44 268,67**
General Expenses	
Bank Charges & Fees	103,65
Salon Rent	7 661,01
Salon Repairs, Maintenance & Upkeep	1 623,09
Gas & Electric	162,45
Telephone & Internet	904,54
Waste Removal	118,42
Advertising/Promotional	4 755,39
Advertising/Promotional	4 755,39
Business Fees, Permits, & Licenses	512,99
Dues & subscriptions	99,98
Insurance	258,00
Meeting Expenses	67,57
Office Supplies	213,59
Personal Protective Equipment	53,39
Salon Technology	1 199,16
Shipping, Freight & Delivery	96,00
Staff Appreciation	405,22
Accounting & Bookkeeping	2 700,00
Coaching/Professional Development	3 208,08
IT - Technical Support	41,16
Admin Wages	7 627,73
Employer Taxes	5 417,36
Salon Training/Continuing Education	799,00
Apprenticeship Program	500,00
Shears Expenses	10,83
Taxes Paid - Sales Tax	222,79
Vehicle Expense	110,25
Total General Expenses	**$38 871,65**
Net Income	**$5 397,02**

FIGURE 12. PROFIT & LOSS REPORT EXAMPLE

The P & L Basics

INCOME

Let's start by going through an actual P & L report for a salon, shown in Figure 12. The first section of your P & L should include all of your *income*–including your service-based income from the salon, any rental income if you rent chairs or suites, your retail income, etc. You want to have a line item for each type of income so you can see how you're doing with each of those streams of income. The income section should be pretty cut and dry.

Income	
Membership Income	5 618.00
Retail Income	15 270.01
Service Income	
Employee Service Income	10.00
Hair Income	57 027.58
Spa Income	10 156.00
Total Service Income	**$67 193.58**
TOTAL INCOME	**$88 081.59**

FIGURE 13. P & L INCOME EXAMPLE

COST OF GOODS (COGS)

Immediately following is your *Cost of Goods Sold* (COGS). Your COGS should include everything that you absolutely must have to produce the product or service that you sell.

Cost of Goods Sold

Backbar - COGS	
Hair BB	2 219.13
Spa BB	969.93
Total Backbar - COGS	**$3 189.06**
Merchant Processing Fees	1 978.88
Retail - COGS	5 328.78
Testers	306.72
Total Backbar - COGS	**$5 635.50**
Service Payroll - COGS	
Hair Wages	20 456.16
Hair Wages - Officer	6 083.25
Spa Wages	6 470.07
Total Service Payroll - COGS	**$33 009.48**
TOTAL COST OF GOODS SOLD	**$43 812.92**

FIGURE 14. P & L COGS EXAMPLE

COGS can be a bit of a gray area for many business owners, but I will define what I consider COGS for a salon or spa for bookkeeping purposes:

- Back Bar (any products used on clients)
- Color Supply (any color used on clients)
- Retail Products
- Payroll & Wages for service providers and technicians
- Merchant Processing Fees
- Service Supplies like capes, combs, foils & aprons

It's vital to break these out into their own line items on your P & L. Look at the example in Figure 14. You don't want these items lumped together because you need to calculate your percentages for each based on industry standards. For example, you need to know your back bar costs compared to your overall sales revenue. That percentage tells us if you are appropriately aligned with industry standards.

In accounting, you take your income minus your COGS, giving you your *gross profit*.

Income – COGS = Gross Profit

However, as you know, there are far more expenses required to run a business than what we see in our COGS.

GENERAL EXPENSES

The third and final section on your P & L report is where we see the rest of your expenses. We call these your *General Expenses,* and they include things like cleaning supplies, repairs, maintenance, upkeep, rent, office expenses, utilities, business supplies–all the things associated with the backend of running a business. If you look at Figure 15, you can see an example of the general expenses on your P & L report.

Expenses
Bank Charges & Fees | 103.65
Facility Expense
  Salon Rent | 7 661.01
  Salon Repairs, Maintenance & Upkeep | 1 623.09
  Utilities
    Gas & Electric | 162.45
    Telephone & Internet | 904.54
    Waste Removal | 118.42
    Total Utilities | **1 185.41**
Total Facility Expense | **$10 469.519**

General Administrative Expenses
Advertising/Promotional | 4 353.40
  Client Appreciation | 217.99
  Market Research | 184.00
Total Advertising/Promotional | **$4 755.39**

Business Fees, Permits, & Licenses
Dues & Subscriptions | 512.99
Insurance | 99.98
Meeting Expenses | 258.00
Office Supplies | 67.57
PPE | 53.39
Salon Technology | 1 199.16
Shipping, Freight & Delivery | 96.00
Staff Appreciation | 405.22
Total General Administrative Expenses | **$7 661.29**

Legal & Professional Services
Accounting & Bookeeping | 2 700.00
Coaching/Professional Development | 3 208.08
IT - Technical Support | 41.16
Total Legal & Professional Services | **$5 949.24**

Payroll Expense
Admin Wages | 7 627.73
Employer Taxes | 5 417.36
Total Payroll Expenses | **$13 045.09**

Payroll Expense
Admin Wages | 7 627.73
Employer Taxes | 5 417.36
Total Payroll Expenses | **$13 045.09**

Salon Training/Continuing Education | 799.00
Apprenticeship Program | 500.00
Total Salon Training/Continuing Education | **$1 299.00**

Shear Expense | 10.83
Taxes Paid - Sales Tax | 222.79
Vehicle Expense
  Fuel Expense | 34.51
  Repair & Maintenance | 75.74
Total Vehicle Expense | **$110.25**

Total Expenses | **$38 871.65**
NET OPERATING INCOME | **$5 397.02**
NET INCOME | **$5 397.02**

FIGURE 15. GENERAL EXPENSES EXAMPLE

Net Income

Lastly, if you look at Figure 12, all the way to the bottom, you will see a final line calculation called *Net Income*. This is where you take the sum of all your income minus your COGS and General Expenses. Whatever you have left over is called Net Income. This number will tell you straight away if the company made more money than expenses for the selected period.

I want to make sure you don't overcomplicate this report, so to keep this as basic as possible, the P & L can be simply defined as:

Income - COGS - General Expenses = Net Income

That is the basic P & L report in a nutshell. Next, let's take a good look at how we can use this report to make some easy, savvy business decisions to increase your net profit.

P & L Profits

Now that you understand the basic layout, I want you to do three essential things that will allow you to start building profits using your P & L instantly.

- Name Each Line Item Correctly
- Put Each Line Item in the Right Place
- Fine Tune Every Line Item for Profits

I can't tell you how often we look at a new client's P & L only to see things like the back bar, color supplies, or even retail all lumped together in their General Expenses. On top of that, many salons that use accounting software just keep the default categories and line-item names that come standard when they set up their new accounts. It's difficult to quickly see where your money is going if you're constantly trying to figure out what each thing stands for. Taking the time to change those category names and line items will save you hours later as you refer to your P & L – which you will be doing as a *Profit First* Salon.

Take a look at the sample P & L in Figure 12. This is a typical setup we use with our Salon Cadence clients. Set up your categories and line items with that sample P & L as a guide, and use the wording and terminology that you currently use in your business. It may seem like common sense, but that is often overlooked. Once you have yours set up this way and you've pulled the report a few times, your business finances will suddenly become so clear and really start to make sense.

What frustrates me is that many hired bookkeepers and accountants don't even change the words to match the business. They will allow the business owner to view these reports completely in the dark. If you have a good bookkeeper (your Tiffany), make sure to work with them and get all the line items set up correctly. If you just take the time to name them properly and put them in the right place on your report, you will be well on your way to having a meaningful P & L report.

The third action item from above is where we start to really impact profitability to make sound business decisions. Here we start fine-tuning everything on your P & L in a way that reduces expenses and increases profits. Nothing on your P & L is untouchable. Believe me, I have found a way to tweak everything on this report. Now, that's a big part of what we do with our clients, and I can't go through every scenario with you here, but the examples below will give you a good idea of how to go about this to get the process started.

Increasing Income

There's no doubt that if you can increase everything in that first *income* section of your P & L, you will have more revenue, and that's a great thing. There are many ways to bring in more clients and increase your productivity. We also need to raise prices from time to time and introduce new and more profitable services into our business. We constantly look at and work on these things in our salon life. I'm not going into detail about it all here since we have already covered much of it throughout other chapters of the book. I just want you to be aware that the income section of the P & L represents the growth of your business.

Now, while increasing income is always a great thing to do, you should equally be looking to cut costs wherever possible. Take another look at our sample P & L in Figure 12. You can see how we start with an income of $88,081 over two months, but by the time service payroll, back bar, retail, and merchant processing fees are taken out, we're left with a *gross profit* of $44,268. Half of our income is gone. And then, after all the general expenses, we're down to a *net income* of $5,397 for the period.

That's only 6% of the salon's income during that time. And while some of you might be thinking you'd love to be making 6% net profit, the reality is that a successful, thriving salon would make far more than that. In fact, our Salon Cadence clients who fall into that same income bracket will aim for 25% to 30% net profit. So, the next logical place we look to increase our net profit is by cutting costs.

Lowering COGS

Many salon and spa owners fall into the mindset that they can't realistically lower their COGS. They believe retail and back bar costs are set, and their hands are tied on how far they can lower those. It's easy to assume that you must have some supply cost to produce income. Well, for sure it's not the easiest thing to do, but if you dig into your costs there, I promise you'll find some room for improvement.

For example, take back bar products related to any product we use on a client to perform our services. First, make sure you differentiate these products from your retail products. Those are two separate things, and you need to be tracking your sole costs of back bar products. Once you see your true back bar expenses, you will instantly start thinking about ways you can reduce some of those costs.

I remember when we realized that we were overutilizing our color when mixing a client application in my salon. Once we realized how much we were spending, I made a conscious effort to reduce the amount of product we used and significantly lowered expenses in that category, and we did that without sacrificing the quality of our color service. But I would never have known we were wasting money in that way if I couldn't see my back bar expenses as a standalone expense on my P & L.

Lowering General Expenses

Much of the time a salon's general expenses are a smart place to get started if you're looking to cut costs. It's much easier to identify things in your general expenses that you can lower or eliminate altogether. It's not uncommon for us to sit with clients and instantly lower their general expenses by 10% in a single session. Imagine what that could do for your bottom line. Let's take a look at some of the low-hanging fruit.

Bank Fees: If you have bank charges and fees showing up every month, they are usually late fees or finance charges on credit cards. Sometimes it's as easy as rescheduling when the payment is due to make it easier with your cash flow. That might be all you need to knock off or lower those extra charges quickly.

Whatever it takes, you really need to make a conscious effort to eliminate those charges. It will be worth it to you in the long run and will save you money. Bank fees and late payments are just money you're giving away to the bank, so that's a good one to dig into and get started with.

Rent: OK, I hear it all the time. You can't change your rent, right? Well, guess what? You're mistaken if you think that because you can. I've had many clients renegotiate the rent or lease terms, instantly boosting their cash flow and net profit. You won't ever know if you don't try. Some landlords have been around a while, and they understand the challenges of running a small business. Lately, many landlords may truly want to help in these challenging times. The last thing they desire is for your business to fail. I'm not saying all landlords have this mentality, but again, you have nothing to lose by having an honest conversation with them.

In addition to rent, you can also look at your utilities, repairs, and upkeep. Obviously, there are things you can't get around, but everything should be looked at. Don't leave any stone unturned. Find lower-cost alternatives if you can and reduce consumption wherever possible. Remember, these little things will add up and return a higher net profit.

Client Appreciation: The client appreciation category includes snacks, tea, coffee, cookies, wine, and any extra things you provide to make the client feel special. While I feel like these are valuable to have within a salon, it is a place to cut some costs.

Advertising and Promotional: You should continually reevaluate any active campaign and look at the return you are getting. Are you bringing enough new clients in from the campaign? Have you increased the amount of retail you're selling or the number of gift cards? What is the goal of your campaign? Are you looking at your return on investment for what you're spending and determining whether it's worth the money you're spending at the time? I see this all the time. Salons run $5,000/month campaigns and only get four or five clients. It's not worth the money that they're spending. Now, if they are getting a bunch of clients, say 50 per month, then of course, it would make sense, but this could be a big area to redirect lost profits, so please take a look.

Dues & Subscriptions: Next, you should look at monthly or yearly recurring dues and subscriptions. See what business software you are using and make sure you really need it and are using it properly. You may be paying for a premium level but only require a basic level. These subscriptions can pile up quickly, so do an inventory and find anything in there you just happen to be paying that you no longer use.

We all do it because we are so connected these days, and before you know it, you have four different music channels, multiple media apps, and competing software platforms. The list goes on, and you forget to cancel things. Some things are once-a-year charges that you forget about, and then they pop up, and it's like, bam, $150 for something you don't need anymore. If you can clean all these up, it saves you money instantly.

Office Supplies: Same thing as above. You should be looking through these charges every month to see if there's anything that you can cut down.

Salon Training: We have our clients watch their salon training because it's an area that adds up fast. Salon owners love education, which is excellent, but I've had clients sign up for something every month and don't have the cash to support it. They are like, "Ooh, I want to take this class and that class and this one," and the next thing you know, they've spent a few thousand dollars. Then, they wonder where their profit went at the end of the month, so if you have a cash flow issue, that's an area to look at and make some choices between which training classes are essential and which are not.

Helpful Tip: If you use QuickBooks, you can click the dollar amount in any category, and it will pull up all the separate charges in there. That makes it easy to see exactly what you're paying for and start making changes. Remember, the goal is to get your net profit up to around 25% of your income. Looking back at the sample P & L we ran for March and April, that is going from $5,400 net profit for those two months to $22,000. Now *that's* the kind of money that can make an impact in your salon!

Summary of P & L: If you set up your report correctly and start using it to cut costs and find profits, the Profit & Loss report will become one of the most valuable tools in your business. I would start by focusing more on the easily changeable things, and hopefully, this overview has given you some good ideas of where to start.

The Balance Sheet

Frequently, people are thrown off when they look at financial reports because they don't understand the difference between a P & L and a Balance Sheet. Just think of it like this, your P & L represents your income and expenses, while your balance sheet numbers represent your company's assets, liabilities, and equity. Let's look at those three things on a balance sheet: assets, liabilities, and equity.

BALANCE SHEET
As of March 31, 2022

	TOTAL
ASSETS	
Current Assets	
Bank Accounts	
Client Drip Account *2748	400,87
Gift Card/Membership Hold *5616	8 495,00
Income *2116	8 801,11
OPEX *2018	35 969,33
Owners Pay *1817	22 973,76
Profit *0913	2 810,92
Profit Hold *2214	12 093,41
Savings *0815	2 170,16
Tax *1016	2 825,80
Tax Hold *1719	21 429,81
Total Bank Accounts	**$117 970,17**
Accounts Receivable	
Accounts Receivable (A/R)	19 729,69
Total Accounts Receivable	**$19 729,69**
Total Current Assets	**$137 699,86**
Fixed Assets	
Furniture & Equipment	440,21
Total Fixed Assets	**$440,21**
TOTAL ASSETS	**$138 140,07**
LIABILITIES AND EQUITY	
Liabilities	
Current Liabilities	
Credit Cards	
AmEx	9 627,57
Total Credit Cards	**$9 627,57**
Other Current Liabilities	
Gift Cards Outstanding	636,77
Payroll Tax Payable - Employees	3 937,25
PPP - Round 2	78 080,00
Sales Tax Payable	2 038,77
Tips Payable	9 091,22
Total Other Current Liabilities	$93 784,01
Total Current Liabilities	**$103 411,58**
Total Liabilities	**$103 411,58**
Equity	
Opening Balance Equity	0,00
Retained Earnings	25 514,54
Shareholder Distribution	-10 515,74
Net Income	
Total Equity	**$14 998,80**
TOTAL LIABILITIES AND EQUITY	**$118 410,38**

FIGURE 16. BALANCE SHEET SAMPLE

Examples of Assets

Bank Accounts: Looking at the sample balance sheet in Figure 16, your bank accounts are the first thing you'll notice in assets. Therefore, any money in any of your bank accounts would be considered an asset in the business. When you follow the *Profit First* system, you will see all those accounts you've set up here: income, profit, owner's pay, tax, OPEX, as well as your two holding accounts, profit hold, and tax hold.

Furniture and equipment: The more expensive furniture and equipment you own, usually items valued above $2,500, will be listed on your balance sheet as an asset. It depends on what your CPA recommends, but typically the higher cost items will go here and will depreciate over the course of a few years or expensed in smaller increments.

As an example of how this might look, let's say your accountant suggests a $2,500 piece of equipment is suitable for five years. They would give you a $500 deductible off your tax return at $500 for five years instead of $2,500 all at once.

Examples of Liabilities

Credit Cards: A good way to think about your liabilities is anything your business owes money to. Your credit cards are always listed as liabilities because you've borrowed money from the credit card company.

Loans: Any loan like an SBA or private loan will be listed as a liability.

Gift Cards: Any gift card that was sold but has not been redeemed will sit as a liability because your client has already made a purchase, but the business still owes the service.

Payroll Tax: This is the tax money that has been collected from employees from their paychecks, but you still owe it to the government.

Tips: Collected tips on credit card sales still owed to the stylist. You likely include their tip money on their paycheck when you do payroll.

One last thing to know is that liabilities fall into two categories: short-term and long-term. Short-term liabilities are things that should be realized in under a year, such as payroll tax and tips. Long-term liabilities are things that will be realized in over a year. For example, if you have bought your building, its mortgage would be paid over several years, making it a long-term liability.

Balance Sheet Equity

Equity is often referred to as shareholders' equity. The "shareholder" could be a single owner, multiple owners, or actual shareholders of the company if your business is set up that way. You can think of shareholder equity as the book value of a company. So basically, equity represents the value that would be returned to a company's shareholders if all of the assets were liquidated and all of the company's debts were paid off.

To put into a simple formula:

Assets - Liabilities = Equity

The type of equity you'll see on the balance sheet is the owner's investments, retained earnings, and net income.

Owner's Investments: Occasionally the salon or spa owner will put money into the company. This is often the case when opening a salon or doing any expansion. This investment will be listed as the owner's equity in the company.

Retained Earnings and Net Income: These calculations show the company's total book value after all expenses have been paid.

Wrap Up

We have covered two crucial financial reports that alone will give you tremendous insight into your company's health. You will be able to make powerful, informed business decisions if these reports are accurate and adjusted to the way you're doing business. Remember to set up all your bank accounts and line items to match our *Profit First for Salons* methodology.

You don't need to over-complicate (or over-think) things. Don't let yourself fall into the "I don't know how to read financials" trap. Just review the reports regularly, and they will begin to make perfect sense. This is such an essential step in building your *Profit First* mindset and one that will pay huge dividends for years to come!

Lastly, make sure to get a great bookkeeper (a.k.a. "Your Tiffany") who is ready and willing to align your books with your *Profit First* system. This will allow you to always have these two reports right at your fingertips anytime you evaluate your business. More importantly, it will give you the ability to fine-tune every aspect of your business for profits.

One of the most incredible things that we have learned through working with Tiffany is that not only do we help our clients implement these strategies, but we also get to practice them together every day in our businesses. Tiffany takes care of our books, and we help her team develop the best practices for salons and spas. Together we walk the walk, and we talk the talk. We hold each other accountable to our mission of helping entrepreneurs become profitable and wealthy so they can live a rich and rewarding life.

At the time of this writing, we have totaled over $2.4 million in profit earnings collectively with our Salon Cadence members. We have seen them fulfill lifelong dreams of buying homes, traveling, giving back to incredible causes, and building scalable businesses so they can enjoy their life knowing that they are financially secure and prosperous.

CHAPTER 9

SALON CADENCE IN MOTION

"I fear not the man who has practiced 10,000 kicks once, but I fear the man who has practiced one kick 10,000 times."
– Bruce Lee

The Burnout Model

I told you how I lived and ran my business in the Burnout Model for many years in an earlier chapter. I'm not alone in this. Most of our Salon Cadence clients live the Burnout Model when they come into our program.

BURNOUT MODEL

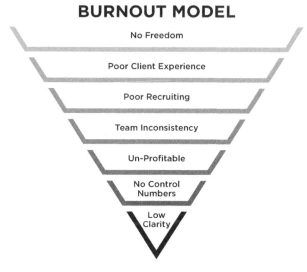

No Freedom

Poor Client Experience

Poor Recruiting

Team Inconsistency

Un-Profitable

No Control
Numbers

Low
Clarity

FIGURE 20. THE BURNOUT MODEL

There is a reason why we burn the candle at both ends and yet still make so little money—because we lack the solid foundation needed to build a strong company. When we start, we have a very low clarity. We don't know exactly what we want. We don't know what our true goals are. We don't understand the numbers and how to drive numbers for success, and, we don't understand profitability. We became unprofitable right from the beginning because we never implemented a profit-based money management system. It's common for new salon owners only to have a vague idea of what they want from running their own business—more time and money freedom, but we have no idea how to make that a reality.

We get so consumed with keeping it all together and working like crazy that we never stop for one second to question why we are doing all of this. We don't stop and ask ourselves if these actions will meet our goals and bring us the life we desire. All this action-taking without a clear vision of where we want to go only leads to burnout.

Due to our uncertainty and inconsistency, our team becomes uncooperative and unmanageable. They are not aligned with the vision of the business, typically because we don't have a clear set of goals, so we can't share them. This leads us to recruit poorly because we do things in a reactionary manner and hire the wrong people. From this point, it's the client's experience that suffers. Even if we're on top of it sometimes, we can't be consistent with the client's experience, so we eventually lose clients. As a result, we have no freedom, weak finances, and no stability. We burn out quickly, just trying to hold it all together. Welcome to the Burnout Model.

Andrea Wintzer's Journey from Burnout to Success

When Andrea (Andi) Wintzer, owner of Studio 16 Salon + Spa in Yakima WA, first came to me, she was near crashing and had been living in the burnout model for a while. She had just experienced a flood in her salon and had to recuperate the repair costs and the financial impact from the loss of days (months actually) that she was closed. She was exhausted and quickly ran through all her funds. When she re-opened the business, she managed to get her and the team up and running and back to full capacity. But while the staff was all making good money, Andi was making nothing. She wasn't taking home a paycheck.

During our first meeting, there was one word she repeatedly said: freedom. More than anything, she wanted to build a company that delivered financial and time freedom for her and her team. Once I'd told her the story of the Starving Stylist and how that lifestyle can be quickly turned around by implementing the *Profit First*, she couldn't wait to get started.

As we began working on the foundations and financials, Andi quickly realized that she was running her company based on other companies in the industry, not by the design of what was right for her business. She had set up her finances and prices based on other salons without regard to her circumstances and profitability. Essentially, her business had been hijacked, and she was too overwhelmed to make any changes.

Realizing all this, we went to work on building a strategy to create the company she envisioned. It didn't take long before Andi completely redesigned her business model and transformed it into a *Profit First* salon. Once she started down that path, she has been profitable ever since. I truly admire her drive and commitment towards her goals, and I'm inspired by her love and dedication to her staff.

When COVID-19 hit, Andi again navigated her company through a very unexpected and unpredictable situation. The difference was that she had *Profit First* working for her. She also had a company that was built and run by design. As a result, she successfully kept her team and profit margin. She even found a way to enhance her business by using her spare time to develop a new sustainable, eco-friendly business model.

Andi continues to be a major contributor to her community. She provides unmatched career opportunities, education, and financial benefits to her team. She spends tons of high-quality time with her grandchildren, son, sister, and mom. She's an avid cyclist and enjoys great Pacific Northwest hiking with her partner. Now *that* is freedom!

The Success Model

Wondering how in the world we were able to help change the entire trajectory of Andi's business so swiftly and easily?

We simply flipped the Burnout Model on its head and rebuilt her business for Success. The only way to create a long-term, scalable business that serves your goals and lifestyle is to understand and implement the Salon Owner Success Model.

OWNER SUCCESS MODEL

Freedom

Legendary
Client Journey

Lifestyle Employment

Team Development

Profit First System

Know Your Numbers

Mindset & Clarity

FIGURE 21. OWNER SUCCESS MODEL

The first three steps of the Success Module are often skipped over because the salon owner feels they need to focus on the team, clients, and branding before anything else. But, it's the first three steps that build the very foundation of your company. Once your strong foundation is set, you can build everything else on top of that. You'll get the right team, clients, and branding because you have a success mindset and clarity on your long-term, strategic vision. This will allow your team to see it as clearly as you and align with it, and soon everything follows and falls right into place.

Start by getting 100% clarity of what you want this business to do for you in terms of professional, social, and financial success. Then, work on sales. Learn how to be efficient with your services. Get your prices right and build profit into every service you offer. Know your numbers inside and out. Then, it's not just knowing how to make money; you'll be set up to keep the money and become profitable by implementing *Profit First*. These are the first three building blocks that will set your business in motion and allow you to build a business by design, a salon that is aligned with the goals you want to achieve.

From there, you can start to focus on the employee journey. You will be so much clearer and know who you want to hire. Recruiting and onboarding become more manageable and successful. Finally, you can set up a legendary client's journey that will attract the right customer. Now you will feel so comfortable putting things together and creating the perfect systems and messaging to develop your business for the long haul.

Putting It All Together

For many years, I suffered from FOMO. It's a terrible thing when your actions are constantly driven by the fear that you're about to miss out or lose something important. For whatever reason, I have gone through most of my adult life with this extreme confidence flaw. As a result of this, I always worked so hard to please everyone, all the time. This was such an extreme challenge because I was in a constant state of working towards perfection. I felt that everything always needed to be perfect so my clients would have a great experience and keep coming back. I designed everything towards the customer's happiness.

I was in this constant state of being there for everybody and every situation. Well, this isn't sustainable. But still, I obsessed over pleasing them all. It got so extreme that I opened my calendar from 8:00 AM to 8:00 PM, six days a week.

My logic went like this: Some clients can only make it to the salon first thing in the morning and need that 8 AM spot. Other clients had to get their kids off to school and then be home after school, so mid-day was best for them. Lastly were the clients who worked all day and needed that late appointment to wind down and get pampered at the end of a long day. So, what did I do? You guessed it—I pleased them all.

I went on like this for years, always accommodating everyone and fitting myself to their needs, living in constant fear that I would lose them if I didn't have the perfect time for them. This became a vicious cycle because it never was perfect. Clients would still need to change their appointments or have some special circumstances that wouldn't work out. My husband kept telling me to be authentic to myself, and that eventually, I wouldn't be able to serve anyone because I'd be too burnt out.

I didn't believe him. I thought something had to be wrong with his logic. As a business owner, I was sure you needed to work 24/7 in the beginning to create customer loyalty and perfection. It took a while, but I finally learned that it just doesn't work that way. Eventually, I realized that you need to know *what you want* from the beginning and then *design your business to work for you.*

If you are conscious of what makes you happy, your clients will follow suit—the same with your team. Everything becomes a reflection of you, and the world adapts around it. Once I got this, I could see how building a successful business had to do less with what my clients needed and more about how the business would work for me and support my life goals. The salon's culture by nature is to uplift others, making them feel beautiful, important, and confident. That is our true gift. If you figure out how to build the model around your goals, you will organically serve your ideal clients with that gift, and they'll love you for it. And you'll do this all while building wealth in your business.

THE SALON CADENCE METHODOLOGY—The Road to Mindset, Wealth, and Freedom

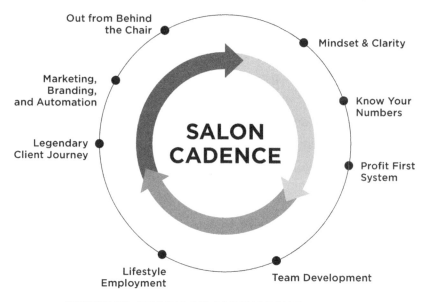

FIGURE 22: THE SALON CADENCE METHODOLOGY

When a new salon owner enters the Salon Cadence program, we always begin with an introduction to our methodology and an overview of what it takes to have true balance and success in your business and life.

We take you through the key elements that it takes to get from being the technician inside your business to the mindset of being the CEO of your business. The Salon Cadence model is designed to define and tighten all your salon systems, building on each other, and creating a platform for you to become a powerful leader. Beyond that, our methodology provides a solid foundation to grow so that you can scale your business.

In this model, the concept of scaling means the business does not rely on your production, time, or income. Even if you choose to continue working as a stylist or aesthetician behind the chair, this approach allows you to create a business that works for you and allows you to grow a successful business that does not depend on you alone.

Here's a quick breakdown of what clients get out of our proven process:

Mindset & Clarity

From the very beginning, we help clients rewire their thinking around what it means to be a successful, profitable salon owner. We know that no matter what systems or processes you put into place, your business will always feel like an albatross around your neck without a successful mindset. After the mindset piece has been shifted, we help you get crystal clear on what you want from your business. We help you discover your purpose and use your gifts to fulfill it and how to create a profitable company through impact. By the end of this, you'll be able to know with certainty: the specific ways your business will support you professionally, socially, and financially, the income you expect and need to live your ultimate life, the amount of time you need to allocate to achieve your goals and ideal lifestyle, the systems you need to implement to make your goals easier to achieve.

The Sales Potential

During the next phase of our methodology, we look closely at your sales and your earnings potential. We'll teach you how to create a successful sales model by maximizing the opportunities at your location. You'll discover how much revenue you can realistically bring in and the most successful revenue-based services that you should focus on to achieve your goals. We'll walk you through learning how to read your numbers so well that you will know every dollar in your business and, more importantly, how to measure your profitability on each of the services you offer.

Profit First

Now that you know your numbers backward and forward, we help you implement the *Profit First* methodology in your business. We use everything you have studied here in *Profit First for Salons* to create an incredible money management system that allows you to build profits, destroy debt, eliminate salon poverty, and become financially sound no matter where you are starting.

Employee Journey

With your finances in place and your profitability growing, you are ready to map out the ideal employee journey that takes a potential team member through an enrollment process, and not any ordinary enrollment process, but one that develops your staff's mindset to work like a shareholder. A shareholder mindset is invested in your business because it aligns with and shares your vision.

Recruiting and Onboarding

From there, we go on the process of recruiting and onboarding. Our clients learn how to identify their ideal staff members and how to recruit them. You'll develop ways to attract your ideal team and create a culture that will have dream employees wanting to work for your company.

Client Journey

Every successful salon must have a legendary client journey. We're going to identify the perfect way to attract your ideal client, learn how to speak to that client, and build long-lasting relationships.

Marketing, Branding, and Automation

Next, we focus on marketing, branding, and automation based on your brand promise to your clients and staff. Once you've determined this, you'll be able to quickly determine the best ways to market your business and services. Then, to top it all off, you'll learn how to automate these systems, so you'll never have to reinvent the wheel.

Out from Behind the Chair

Finally, you learn how to step out from behind your chair to become the owner, not the operator, of your business. You will understand the concept of running your business as the CEO of your company and finally enjoy the time and financial freedom that made you start your business in the first place.

After working with hundreds of salon owners, we've found that to own a successful, thriving salon, you must have a complete strategy that encompasses all these critical areas of your business. They are the key building blocks to developing a solid foundation in your business. In short, you need a powerful mindset, a wealth-building system, and time freedom to live a fulfilled, successful salon entrepreneurial life. It's the combination of all these things that will allow you to create a company that serves your lifestyle, goals, and mission. We invite you to learn how we can support you in building the business you've always dreamed of by visiting SalonCadence.com.

If you're wondering if Salon Cadence is really as good as we say, don't just take our word for it. See what our clients have to say:

"Pre-Salon Cadence, I worked long hours trying to figure out the system that would show me a healthy profit after all my hard work. I entered business ownership to have freedom, but I experienced the opposite. I thought it had to be a long, arduous path towards a reward in the distant future. If I work hard enough, I'll see the reward. That was my old way of thinking.

The *Profit First for Salons* approach is the quickest transformation I've witnessed monetarily. Hiring Salon Cadence was the most important decision I've ever made in my business. Ronit and Salon Cadence have designed the perfect educational pathway into understanding *Profit First* as it relates to our industry. With that foundational support, you start to operate your business on clarity and purpose. I now understand my exact cost-per-hour and how to drive my influencing factors and industry benchmarks. My business no longer runs my life; I'm in the driver's seat, and that is priceless. Now I have the time, strategies, and financial peace of mind I desired when I started my salon."

Lorraine Masters of Ambiance Spa & Salon

"Before I started Salon Cadence, my biggest struggle was knowing how to read and understand my financial numbers. I didn't know whether I was making money, losing money, or breaking even. I never seemed to have the time to look at my numbers, let alone dive into them, because I was afraid to discover where I was. Implementing the *Profit First for Salons* method has helped me focus on my financial status. Setting aside time weekly to allocate my funds keeps me on track and encourages me to maintain a close relationship with my numbers.

I was fortunate to meet Ronit six months into my entrepreneurial adventure. Since then, I have opened a second salon and no longer rely on my time behind the chair to pay the bills. I can focus most of my time on growing and building my team. With my ability to invest my time into them, they, in turn, are thriving. I look forward to buying a home for my family and helping those who have endured domestic abuse. Now that I have the tools to grow my business's profit margin, I will have the means to donate and partner with nonprofits around my community to do just that."

Leanne Stephens of Jade Fox Beauty

"I was struggling to come up with new ideas to do the same things when starting the Salon Cadence program. I have owned Glow for 19 years, and as a business owner, it is easier to go on autopilot when something is working well enough rather than shake things up to see better results. Financially, I was in good shape, but I knew I needed to dive deep into my numbers to squeeze out every last drop of profitability and examine where all the money was going. I love the cost of services analysis – it is unique to you and your circumstances. It was a huge eye-opener.

Now I only work behind the chair one day a week, and I enjoy it fully! If I don't want to work on clients, I have that ability. The salon is not reliant on my income. I do it because I love what I do. Salon Cadence keeps you focused on what is essential —client happiness, team happiness, cash flow management, expenses (including taxes) accounted for, planned bonuses—all while working less!

As an entrepreneur, it can get lonely. You are expected to have all the answers. But in Salon Cadence, we are all focused on working smarter, not harder. We support one another and don't let each other get away with excuses that keep us from our highest and best selves."

Shelly North of Glow Beauty Boutique

"When I came to Salon Cadence, I was exhausted, mentally, physically, and emotionally. I had read *Profit First*, and it spoke to me, but I wasn't about to commit to a whole new anything. After spending some time with Ronit, I knew I had to join her coaching program if anything was going to change. I learned to save for a rainy day and watch my budget like a NINJA. Before joining, my biggest stressor was cash flow - it was flowing out and not in. I was making decisions based on emotion. Now, I approach decisions with data first, not feelings.

Creating a real plan was both difficult and rewarding. The reward started showing up so fast, I couldn't believe it. I had two months of rent saved and money set aside for taxes within six months! I would not have made it through the never-ending shutdowns of 2020 and 2021 if it were not for Ronit and the *Profit First for Salons* methodology. I have reduced my BTC time to 15 hours a week and now have time to work ON my business. I have the time to think and let my creative brain surface again. I get to spend quality time on myself and with the ones I love. I can't say enough about Ronit and Salon Cadence!"

Andi Wintzer of Studio 16 Salon

"When I started with Salon Cadence, I was a single parent to a oddler, going through a surprise divorce, and in the middle of the pandemic. I had the guts to make it, but I knew I needed people in my corner to boost me in business. The most rapid growth change I saw after working with Ronit was structure, organization, and money! More money. It's magic when you surround yourself with like-minded people in your industry who believe you can prosper in bigger ways than you can imagine. Ronit helped me feel business smart—I was no longer just winging it. I can't say enough about the value in the gift of feeling like I CAN DO THIS!

I'm still doing a lot of hustling because I'm not in the phase yet of being the full-time CEO of my business, but I'm in the process. I have purchased a home with a large lump sum down payment in just a year and am working on my second salon expansion. I've been able to cut back on behind the chair hours and am spending more quality time with family and able to block off in advance for vacations! That is the power of community. That is the power of coaching!"

Becky Phelps of Shine Hair Design

"My biggest struggle was my headspace when I started working with Salon Cadence. I was always too busy to give myself the time to figure out how I wanted to live my life and how I could influence others to do what they did best and not try to do it all myself. After working with Ronit, I quickly learned to create new weekly/daily routines. She opened my eyes to *Profit First* and how I could shift from worrying about money to having a plan for the money and the ability to save for the company's future growth. This system gave me hope that all my hard work would pay off to become a profitable and sustainable company! I can breathe now, knowing I have cash flowing into my profit and taxes account and other reserves. I save lots of time not juggling money every week. Working with Salon Cadence, I evolved from thinking I had to do everything from cutting hair to managing daily operations. In fact, I was hurting the company by stretching myself so thin. I love to visualize the future and create opportunities for others. Ronit opened my mind to how a CEO runs a company that is organized and well thought out. I now get more time with my family in our dream home!"

Scott Allison of S Salon

"I was just barely making it when I joined Salon Cadence. I had implemented a few of the *Profit First* practices, but not nearly enough of them. Ronit helped me finish what I had started. She held me accountable and put me on the right path. The *Profit First for Salons* technique makes accounting easier. I actually started paying myself when I started using it. Before that, my mindset was, "Well, whatever's left is what I pay myself." Having the spreadsheet and breaking everything down in my allocations makes life so much easier. Thanks to the *Profit First for Salons* methodology taught in the Salon Cadence program, I've finally retired from behind the chair. I spend my time working on my business, and I have a lot of money saved for building renovation. These plans would not be possible today without the implementation of *Profit First for Salons.*"

Jenna Bowden of Crown Salon and Extension Studio

"Before working with Ronit in the Salon Cadence program, I felt like I was on a bit of an island without enough resources. I'd begun to question if there was a better way that would provide the income I anticipated. Everything shifted for me and my business once I began focusing on revenue and profit-per-hour. Now, I have the confidence that I have enough direction and resources to succeed."

Nick Bennett of Zaza Salon and Spa

CHAPTER 10

THE RIDE TO FREEDOM

"Your current situation is not your final destination. Press on!" –
Dr. Leon Alexander

My friend and mentor, Neil Ducoff, rode in the MS Cape Cod Getaway for several years. It's a 2-day bike ride from Boston to Provincetown on Cape Cod—160 miles. That route would go right past my house every year at the end of June, and one year, I met Neil at a rest stop to cheer him on with some food and beverages. While we chatted at the rest stop, Neil told me that I'd be riding with him next year. Since I can never turn down a challenge, I decided to go for it. After all, I'd have a whole year to prepare, so why not?

I remember training for that ride like it was yesterday. For an entire year, I dedicated time and energy to riding and educating myself about the sport of cycling and understanding the basics. And finally, after a long year of anticipation, the day of the ride arrived. Well, let me tell

PROFIT FIRST FOR SALONS

you, I never expected how hard it would be. Even after all my effort, I quickly discovered that I wasn't prepared for the grueling ride.

It took me eight hours to complete the first day, more than two hours behind my team. I finally got to the finish line, and everyone else in the group cheered me on when I arrived at our final destination. It felt good to finish, but it was bittersweet. I had already made up my mind that Day 2 wasn't going to happen for me—I was going to pull out of the ride.

I may sound like a broken record, but it takes tremendous focus and determination to achieve your goals. Case in point: I wanted so badly to be part of the team that promotes this ride for my friends and clients and to have that one extra achievement to be proud about. I wasn't ready for this ride because I hadn't focused on what mattered most: getting results and completing the two-day challenge.

As much as I felt dejected from dropping out, I couldn't sign up fast enough for the following year. Determined to make up for that first year, I took a whole new approach in my training. This time around, all my preparation was aligned with finishing both days. But it was even more than that, I wanted to finish strong with a respectable time. I did everything I could to start building a team around me that was 100% in sync with my goals.

I even enlisted my husband, Bill, to get a bike and train with me. Bill is naturally more athletic than me, so he was a great motivator and encouraged me to keep pushing when I wanted to stop. He challenged me to compete with him, though we both knew I was no competition. Day after day, I was challenged with negative thoughts about my skills, especially compared to Bill's. I had to confront endless negative self-talk like, "I'm not good enough," "I shouldn't be doing this," "I won't be able to finish," or "I'm simply not strong enough." Yet, Bill pushed and pulled me along until I finally felt comfortable with the idea that completing the two-day ride was doable.

When the day of the ride finally arrived, I knew I had this. We had trained so hard and so strategically. It was now just a matter of going out there and executing the plan. I kept envisioning myself completing the ride and rewarding myself with something special after I'd crushed my goal.

The starting line felt familiar. In my mind, I repeated the mantra of the little engine that could from the children's book classic (I think I can, I think I can, I know I can, I know I can). Racing ahead past the starting line with intention and purpose, I had a great morning keeping pace with my team. At about the 40-mile mark, I started to drop back to pace myself, which was part of the strategy to have a successful first day.

A few miles later, there was a break area where sponsors of the race provided water and energy packs to refresh riders along the strenuous route. I decided to continue past that stop because I knew of a bakery further up ahead that had a very convenient outdoor restroom, so I hurried ahead.

When I reached the bakery, that old familiar troublemaker called "adversity" hit me like a ton of bricks. Just as I got off the bike, my shoe got jammed in the pedal clip, and down I went. I tried to balance myself and brace for the fall at the same time, but unsuccessful at either, I fell awkwardly on the metal stairs leading to the restroom entry. Immediately, intense pain shot through the bottom of my rib cage. Once I could catch my breath through the pain, I saw a gash in my knee, oozing blood. Still high on adrenaline, a quote from my favorite Monty Python movie popped into my head, "Merely a flesh wound!" I certainly hadn't gone through all this to let a few bumps and bruises stop me. So, I went to the bathroom, got back on my bike, and started to pedal.

With this snafu under control, I was back on my bike and continued toward the 75-mile finish line and that ultimate prize I was planning to reward myself with when I completed the second day. There were a couple of big hills on the horizon, and as I approached the first one, I stood up on my bike to get a little more traction to push up the steep slope. I sucked in a breath when an agonizing, sharp pain ripped through the side of my abdomen.

As I allowed gravity to pull me down the hill, Bill called to see how I was doing. Still cringing from that sharp pain, I gave him the abridged version of my fall and asked him if I should keep going. With major hesitation in his voice, he encouraged me to keep going. We agreed that I'd rethink the decision if the pain got worse after a few more miles. So, with that boost of encouragement, I kept going. The next 30 miles or so were somewhat brutal. There were lots of hills, up and down, up and down. I doubled up on GU (an energy gel) and popped several Advil. It was less than three hours to get to that Day 1 finish line, and I was determined to make it.

Later that afternoon, I met up with my riding partner Nicole at a triage area set up for riders. One trained medical professional checked me over and gave me an ice pack to apply to my right side. I had a few scratches but was released to prepare for the next day's ride. By the time I showered and arrived at my room, I was in even more pain than before. I lied down, popped more Advil, and decided to celebrate finishing Day 1 by crashing in bed early with hopes I would somehow be ready for that second day.

Why People Don't Make It and Why You Will

There are a few reasons why people don't make it to the finish line. Here are the reasons and how you can shift your thinking and actions to win the game of business and success.

Crystal Clear Vision

Several times throughout the night, I debated in my head whether I should continue with Day 2 of the ride. But after much thought, my vision of finishing this ride was too strong to let go. The following day, I was up and at the starting line for the 4:30 am start. At this point, there was no more negotiating. Pain or no pain, my mind was made up to cross the finish line. Steeling myself, I thought about my special reward and visualized the finish line. I focused on my understanding of how the brain is a goal-achieving machine—the minute you give it a goal, it will do whatever it takes to get you there if you're focused. It was off to the races—here I come, Day 2.

Most of us lack the kind of vision in our business that we have in the other areas of our lives. For many business owners, the vision is often blurred, and little by little, we drift away from our goals. Our course becomes diverted until we end up just changing our direction.

Do you ever ask yourself what you want to get out of it? How does this business that I am building work for my personal, professional, and spiritual goals? It's essential to remind yourself of your ultimate purpose and end vision. Mine was to finish 160 miles in two days. That was a pretty clear vision. In contrast, my biggest mistake while owning a salon is that it took me many years to establish my end game vision.

If you have a hard time getting to that clarity, here are a few steps that will help you get there.

Map It Out

Nothing is more important than having a detailed roadmap. This includes writing out small goals for each step and adding timelines, so it's clear what needs to be accomplished by when. When faced with a difficult task, it can be hard to stay motivated. Old habits die hard, and new ones take time, but if you break your goals into smaller pieces rather than try for the whole thing at once, success becomes much more attainable!

My first ride took me eight hours to finish. The following year, I improved that time to seven hours (while dealing with an injury through half the ride). The difference is that I had a roadmap with milestones, and I knew where I was going. I planned everything from where I would stop for breaks to the exact pace that I needed to keep to make it through the day.

Well, it was no different when it came to running my business. Once I learned to map out my days, weeks, and months, I started to have immediate results. For example, every Monday I would have two hours cleared on my calendar just for financials and reviewing my profit plan. That allocation of time was critical to achieving my revenue goals.

I also created a 12-month map with the precise financial goals I needed in my business. Each month had its own subset of goals with clearly defined steps. I knew exactly when and how I would accomplish each and every milestone. I scheduled it all in my calendar, and I never deviated from it. I was determined to keep that going, and I still do it today. I plan for everything in my calendar, including vacation days, creative thinking days, monthly allocations and bank transfer days, quarterly distributions, etc. Everything I can think of gets planned in my calendar, and that's my roadmap to success.

Momentum and Keeping Your Eye on The Prize

When you train for a cycling competition, you have to find your ride and speed. As you climb up a hill, you pedal fast on a lower gear, and as you reach the top, you squeeze and push on a higher gear. Once you are on the top, you pick up speed down the hill and get great momentum. It's so much fun coasting down, but if you want to last the ride, you have to get back into that cadence again once the coasting is finished. You do this over and over so that you maintain your momentum throughout the ride.

The same is true with your business and with the *Profit First* system. To make those long-term gains and build that big profit account, you must keep your momentum. It's not rocket science, and believe me, it works. There is a reason that we see thousands of small businesses growing consistently and profitably by following this methodology. It all has to do with building and maintaining momentum.

Stop Your Zigzagging

It takes 15 days to form a new habit, 21 days to maintain it, and 90 days to make it into a lifestyle. Don't fall off track—take the 90-day challenge and change your life. We have free resources waiting for you at ProfitFirstSalons.com to make it easier to meet and crush that challenge. You will also have the opportunity to join our private group of profitable salons and spas, so you can keep your positive mindset working for you.

Commit to building a roadmap and hang it somewhere you'll see it every day and know exactly where you are going. If you fall off the bike, get back on and keep riding. Learn to trust the process. Remember what Mike says, "Profit is not an event. Profit is a habit." I'll go one step further and tell you this: Profit is a lifestyle!

Fried Clams

I started this chapter recanting my attempts at completing a two-day bike ride that my mentor suggested. Well, after two years of intense training, I pushed up and down 15 hours of hills to cross the finish line on Day 2. On the wings of clarity, I mastered the challenge. At the end of that ride, across from the finish line in Provincetown, Cape Cod, there was a lobster house with the special reward I had envisioned for 160 miles. What could have channeled my vision with such clarity and tempestuous delight? Fried clams. Yep, you read that right. I trained hard and ate clean for an entire year with a vision of crossing the finish line and eating fried clams at the end of the journey.

What I didn't know was that my fall at the bakery had caused much more than a flesh wound. A few days after the bike challenge, I found out that I had been riding with three broken ribs, one that had shifted close to my lungs. Though I would never suggest you put your health in jeopardy, I am suggesting nothing is more potent than having 100% clarity and focus on your goals. When you are so committed that you can *feel* the exhilaration of crossing that finish line, you'll find that even the most challenging obstacles can be minimized to nothing more than a bump in the road.

How Jenna Bowden Got It Right

When I first met Jenna Bowden, owner of Crown Extension Studio in Colorado Springs, CO, she had already implemented the *Profit First* methodology in her business. So naturally, I was excited when she enrolled in our coaching program at Salon Cadence. Getting to know Jenna has been an incredible pleasure. She is a fierce leader, and when she believes in something or someone, she goes all in and plays all out. She was already dedicated to *Profit First* and made regular allocations to her profit account. Jenna started with *Profit First* about six months before COVID-19 hit the U.S., so she had some significant momentum leading up to her salon being closed during the lockdown. Her profit account helped her stay in business during those difficult months of the pandemic.

When I started coaching Jenna, I looked at her books and discovered that she wasn't using the full methodology and was missing out on quite a bit of potential. After digging into her finances, we found her bookkeeping was way off and didn't match up with her *Profit First* accounts. This is typical of many salons I work with. Sometimes, you just don't know what you don't know.

Jenna was excited and determined to get things in order. We immediately helped her clean up the books and align everything with *Profit First*. After just those tiny tweaks, Jenna's *Profit First* assessment showed an increase of over 15% in profit and owner's pay and a 10% decrease in unwelcomed expenses.

Although Jenna lost several employees due to COVID-19's impact on her salon, she not only endured, but she also thrived. She continued to increase profits and owner's pay and built a new hiring and recruiting system simultaneously. I can't wait to see what's next for Jenna. I know her vision, mission, and core values, and she has become quite the unstoppable force.

The Future of Salons

During and after COVID-19, we encountered overnight challenges and long-term changes. It became a domino effect of events that changed the course of salons for good. In the first few months following the re-opening of our salons, many clients were very hesitant to schedule appointments. For many salons, it wasn't easy to convince people that it was safe to come back to the salon physically.

Many salons offered home-based products to keep revenue coming into the business during the shutdown. Suddenly, it became easier for many clients to stay at home and continue their new routine. New wardrobe companies came about with Zoom clothing lines and advised how to show up for Zoom. Before you know it, we all were living the Zoom MODA: beautiful hair, makeup, and jewelry combined with pajama pants and slippers.

Salons were suddenly marketing in new ways to get clients back into their stores, employing playful marketing strategies that spoke to the Zoom clients. We needed strong messaging and promises of safety in the chair. Once it caught on, old clients started swarming back, and we saw an influx of new clients. The new game was how to master the retention of new clients.

The next challenge became staffing. Employees from both commission salons and hourly-based salons started to drift. Many stylists who lost their jobs started turning to salon suites. Other team members didn't want to come back to work for various reasons. Some had kids at home when schools were closed. Others realized they wanted to have more flexibility in their lives and wanted to work on their own.

It became complicated to find, recruit, and retain our staff. It was an unforeseen phenomenon with new and old clients coming in, yet not nearly enough staff to handle the demand. Unless you saw it coming and prepared financially for it, you became overwhelmed. Your skeleton crew started feeling burnt out and exhausted. Many salon owners lost their hold on their team, and many employees left or disengaged. They were hanging around watching the economy before determining their next move.

Now more than ever, salon owners and managers must learn to understand the needs of their future workforce. You can choose to be bitter or better. In Salon Cadence, we believe in utilizing this remarkable new generation of stylists as your community. The "Lifestyle Employment," as we call it, is about creating a team of shareholder-minded employees. We teach salon owners how to fully commit to understanding what stylists want and need and what makes them tick. Once you understand this, you need to prepare for it and build the systems and strategy to make it all work. It may sound like a lot, but I promise it's easier than you think, and we have some great resources to get you started. It's all available online at ProfitFirstSalons.com.

But before you jump right in, let me explain the single most crucial part of building a "Lifestyle Employment" salon. You must have the right financial model in place to support it. You must have *Profit First* up and running. If you've read this book all the way here, this should come as no surprise. Simply put, without having the *Profit First* system in place, you will never be able to support your financial or employment goals. To grow, you need a simple way of planning your profits and building the savings you'll need for recruiting and supporting the right team in this new climate.

Our Salon Cadence clients use *Profit First* to remove the guessing and strategically prepare to recruit great talent. Most of our clients add one more bank account to the system called "Lifestyle Employment." Yes, yes, I know one more account. I can see you rolling your eyes, but I have to say it's building rockstar teams across the salon industry. Allocate just 5% from your INCOME into this account once you get settled into your new routine. Don't do this initially, instead focus on building the core *Profit First* system. Think of this as Phase 2 in your new money management lifestyle.

Your Profit First Lifestyle, Phase 2

During an interview I had with my good friend, and brilliant professor, Dr. Henrik Totterman of Hult International Business School, he summarized perfectly the value of running your business with a profitable mindset:

> "Businesses that flourish have a healthy rainy-day savings account. Although we don't know exactly what is around the corner, we can always expect the unexpected. For example, during the COVID-19 shutdowns, the businesses that thrived had enough cash flow to sustain them. They didn't know it would be specifically COVID-19 that would cause such uncertainty in the market, but they understood that something would because it always does, and they made sure they were ready for it.
>
> Having this rainy-day fund allows a business to be nimble and agile. Businesses that prosper during challenging times are always the ones that can pivot quickly by being innovative and creative. But to be innovative, we must allow ourselves as business owners enough time in our creative genius.
>
> Many business owners never reach the place of nimbleness and true financial security because they don't look creatively at how they could innovate in their business. They instead waste time in the minutia of their business rather than delegating things that aren't necessary for them to do. If business owners allow themselves time to spend in creative flow, they will be in a better place financially. They will

be innovative before they need to pivot because of unexpected societal changes or their industry."

Excerpt from my Interview with Dr. Henrik Totterman from Hult International Business School

You can advance your lifestyle by incorporating *Profit First* into any size salon, whether you are a salon owner or a solo stylist building your career. The *Profit First* system will get you there even if you're a stylist with your own salon suite who wants to work less and make more.

Maybe you are a salon that wants to grow to high six or seven figures. In either case, this system will get you there. You can utilize the *Profit First* system in every area of your business. At this writing, over 200,000 businesses are using this method, and so should you.

I am often asked when a salon owner should start using *Profit First*. My answer always is, "How quickly do you want to be profitable?" I'm not trying to be smart-alecky, but seriously, how about right now? Who doesn't want to start building profits immediately? And here is the great thing about starting today: You can also apply the same principles to your personal finances when you learn this method. That's right, Bill and I have an entire *Profit First* system for our home banking. And guess what? Our profit account is enormous! Once you get the cadence for *Profit First* at home, you can start multiplying your wealth by investing in other areas like the stock market, cryptocurrency, real estate, and other investments.

Here is one more great thing to think about - once you get up and running, you can take it to a higher level and incorporate this teaching and learning with your staff. Build a self-development and money management education department in your salon to teach your staff how to use *Profit First*. What a great tool to teach your staff - how to manage their money and show them the power of investing in their life, career, and dreams.

Now, as I mentioned before, you can implement this book on your own, and you can start a life of profitability today (and you should). But if you want to accelerate your learning, then take one extra step and check out the free resources at our website, ProfitFirstSalons.com. You'll find worksheets and downloadable resources to help you throughout each step of the process. In addition, you will have the opportunity to learn more about the coaching and community we provide to salon owners and beauty professionals.

In Closing

I want to say that it has been a pleasure sharing my journey with you and all the great stories of our amazing clients. *Profit First* has changed my life and so many others around me. Being part of this community has become a way of life for me, and I want that for you too. Our industry is beaming with creativity and many strong and gifted people. Together, we are an incredible force and bring so much good into this world.

I am committed to seeing that energy and passion continue to grow and thrive for years to come. The endless opportunities are right there in front of us. We just need the right tools. As I mentioned earlier, you can't build a great home without a solid foundation. When it comes to your salon and spa business, that foundation is *Profit First*.

Therefore, I'm urging you one last time, *"don't wait another minute"* to get started. Do it today and set your sights on the highest level of success you can imagine. Build your roadmap and go for your dreams.

I'm here for you, so please reach out with comments and feedback and let me know how you're doing in your journey. I honestly can't wait to hear from you.

To your success!

Cheers,

Ronit

ACKNOWLEDGMENTS

When my friend Nicole sent me one of her go-to books, *Profit First,* by Mike Michalowicz, I couldn't wait to start reading it. I'd read his first book, *The Toilet Paper Entrepreneur,* when I was running my salon, and it changed the way I understood cash flow in my business. *Profit First* offered me the simple system I'd been searching for to make my salon truly profitable for years. Finally, my business finances made sense. After devouring *Profit First,* I put the entire system into place and started seeing amazing results. That's when I realized that I could help other entrepreneurs with businesses like mine with this simple formula. I knew then that I wanted to write *Profit First for Salons* under Mike's brand.

In 2019, I started the writing process, believing the book would be ready for publication by 2020. But, like so many things when the pandemic hit, I put the book on the back burner. To say I was disappointed would be a huge understatement.

In hindsight, I believe that putting the publication on hold was a blessing in disguise. Now it contains case studies of salons that were able to thrive while experiencing the most challenging times in our industry. Not only do we have cases that prove the system is super efficient, but also that it works, even when all around us salons were closing their doors for good. Our Salon Cadence coaching clients stuck to the system the whole time and not only managed the challenges but *actually grew* _their profits!_ Simply put, the methods outlined in _Profit First for Salons_ have never been so essential.

I'd like to dedicate this book to all the people who supported me in the process and inspired me to write it. To my girlfriend and life buddy, Shelley North, who kept pushing me, knowing what a huge financial and time investment it was. Writing a book is like giving birth. Through wins and losses, you have been my feedback flight attendant, partner in travel, and co-conspirator in the entrepreneurial adventure. I am grateful that you had faith in me to build Salon Cadence and share your vision of bringing _Profit First_ to our industry.

To my friend, Frank Fulco, who has the biggest serving heart and is one of the most committed and laser focused people I know. His passion for our industry is like gold dust. More than anything, for believing in me and giving me a platform to bring my message to the world every week.

To Erin Morgan, my guide from _Profit First_, who believed that I was the best person in the industry to write this book.

To Anna Walsh and Amy Roland, my first Salon Cadence clients who still remain committed to the journey

To Andrea Wintzer and Scott Allison for believing in the method and working so hard to implement it.

To Llacey Simmons, my amazing copy editor, who turns my voice into magic words.

To Larthinia Howard, our writing coach, who helped us gather our thoughts and write the first draft.

To Jacqueline Myers, our brilliant editor, who took the rough manuscript and helped us bring words, meaning, and facts together in the best way to help you understand the concepts.

To Mike Michalowicz, thank you for being our guide for this brainchild, allowing me to write it, and believing in us (I know you had many people wanting to write the book).

To all my salon and spa friends who pushed me to bring this to life. We can help all of you become a part of the top 2% in the industry and change the profit story of so many.

To my children, Gabi and Will, and son-in-law Brandon, thanks for putting up with me all these years being an entrepreneurial mom and forgiving me for missing so many of your important events while I built my companies. And finally, for pushing me to always move forward during tough times. You are the reason I push forward; you are my inspiration.

Most importantly, I want to dedicate the success of completing *Profit First for Salons* to my husband, Bill Enos. Bill documented and captured my voice and teachings as if I were writing the book. To capture my voice, Bill interviewed me, wrote the story, and translated many of Mike's chapters to our *Profit First for Salons*. Together, we met several times with Mike and got his guidance on the book and cross-channeled our ideas. Bill implemented our true real-time stories and the experience through the eyes of our clients.

RESOURCES

When you buy *Profit First for Salons,* you immediately gain access to our library of resources. (Profit First for Salons is more than just a book…)

All you have to do is open your camera on your smartphone, hover over these QR Codes, and click the website links!

Profit First for Salons - Resources
URL: ProfitFirstSalons.com

 Scan me and get access to these downloads: Allocation Calculator, Calculating Salon Profit Per Hour, Profit Assessment Worksheet & Examples, Salon Owner Burnout & Success Models, Sample Balance Sheet, Sample Profit & Loss, and more!

Salon Cadence - Website
URL: SalonCadence.com

 Scan me and get access to the Salon Cadence website mentioned in the book! Learn about our salon business coaching, find beauty business blogs, hear from our heroes, and learn about our amazing team. See first hand what makes us a white-glove experience.

Ronit Enos - Website
URL: RonitEnos.com

 Scan me and get access to the inside scoop on Ronit's personal blogs, workshops, speaking events, business & wellness retreats, and all the work she's been doing.

Profitable Salon and Spa Owners - Facebook Group

 Scan me and get access to our worldwide networking experience! Join our Facebook group and meet like-minded beauty business owners from all over the world who are looking to reach the top 5% of earners in our industry.

Made in the USA
Las Vegas, NV
08 February 2024

85440358R00104